Anatomy of the
Harley-Davidson

The Anatomy of the
Harley-Davidson

John Carroll

Regency House Publishing Ltd.

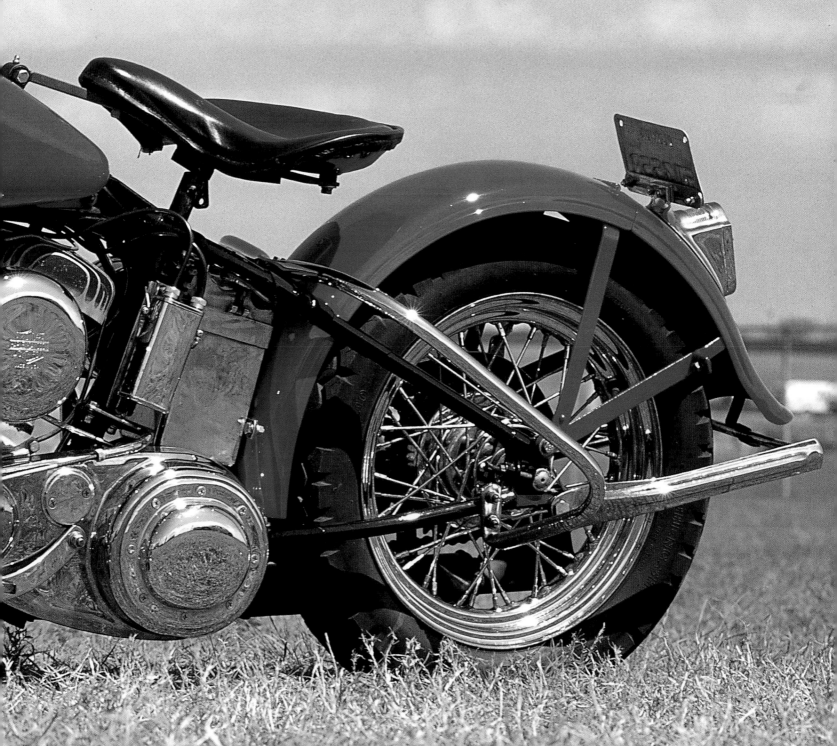

Pages 2-3
A 1945 WLA 45.

Right
Springer forks were superseded in 1948.

Opposite
A Shovelhead of the AMF era.

Page 6
An Evo Electra Glide.

Page 7
A 1948 WL.

ALL PICTURES ARE SUPPLIED BY KIND PERMISSION OF GARRY STUART. ILLUSTRATIONS ARE BY LOUISE LIMB.

Published in 1997 by
Regency House Publishing Limited
3 Mill Lane
Broxbourne
Hertfordshire
EN10 7AZ
United Kingdom

**Copyright © 1997
Regency House Publishing Limited**

ISBN 1 85361 455 6

Printed in China

CONTENTS

Foreword

The surnames of two families, Harley and Davidson, European immigrants to the United States, combined to form the brand name of some of the most recognized motorcycles in the world. The Harley-Davidson is more than just a motorcycle – it is an American icon, the embodiment of America on two wheels. The attentions of Hollywood's film makers has no doubt helped Harley-Davidson achieve such a status with classic films such as Easy Rider and Electra Glide in Blue prominent among a host of other motorcycle movies.

There is a huge amount of jargon associated with Harley-Davidsons, so in order to elucidate for those new to the marque, a few pointers to describe the various types follow. There are the 'Flatheads', built between 1909 and 1973 in various capacities including 45-, 55-, 74- and 80-cubic inch displacements; 'Knuckleheads', overhead valve machines built from 1936 to 1947 in 61- and 74-cubic inch displacements; 'Panheads', updated overhead valve machines built between 1948 and 1965 in 61- and 74-cubic inch sizes; the 'Generator Shovelheads', built in 74-cubic inch displacement but only between 1966 and 1969; the 'Alternator Shovelheads', manufactured from 1970 to 1983 in 74- and 80-cubic inch displacements; the 'Sportsters' made from 1957 to date in 55-, 61- and 74-cubic inch displacements. However, the story of Harley-Davidson is much more than one of capacities and model designations as one or two of the nicknames above might indicate.

INTRODUCTION

The history of the Harley-Davidson marque is both long and proud and begins in the first years of the 20th century. The beginnings of the now-mighty company were distinctly humble; in 1903, two of the Davidson brothers, Arthur and Walter, and William S. Harley built a single-cylinder motorcycle in their spare time that displaced approximately 10 cu in (160cc). It worked well enough, though lacking in hill-climbing ability, but encouraged the group to build two improved motorcycles in 1904 with the intention of selling them. The Davidson brothers' Aunt Janet pinstriped the finished machines prior to their sale. From then on the company was in business and production grew exponentially; in 1905 the group made eight motorcycles, in 1906 50, 150 in 1907 and over 400 in 1908. Their first factory was a shed built by the Davidsons' father and the third Davidson brother, William A., joined the fledgling company which filed its incorporation papers in 1907. The company that was to become so famous was in business and would stay under the control of the Harley and Davidson families until 1969 when American Machine and Foundry (AMF) bought the company.

The early V-twin Harleys, such as this 1913 model photographed in California (above), featured a clutch in a primary case (opposite above) and suspension in the forks. The springs were shrouded (opposite below).

1906 Silent Gray Fellow

The Silent Gray Fellow was so named because of its quiet running, as a result of its muffler, and the Renault grey paint schemes. The engine size of the model was sequentially increased from 405cc (25 cu in), when introduced, to 500cc (30 cu in) in 1909 and to 565cc (35 cu in) in 1913. Other changes made in the duration of the production run were to the design of the cylinder-head cooling fins and a reshaping of the front downtube of the frame. The gas tank was redesigned in 1912 and 1916 while belt drive was discontinued in 1914. Production of all singles ended in 1918 with the trend towards V-twins by American manufacturers. V-twins were seen as a way of increasing the power of a motorcycle engine cheaply and the design fitted existing frames.

Technical Specification 1906 SILENT GRAY FELLOW	
Capacity	25 cu in (405cc)
Engine Cycle	Four stroke
Engine Type	One cylinder
Valve configuration	Inlet over exhaust
Top Speed	50 mph (80 km/h)
Power	n/a
Transmission	Single speed
Frame	Steel loop

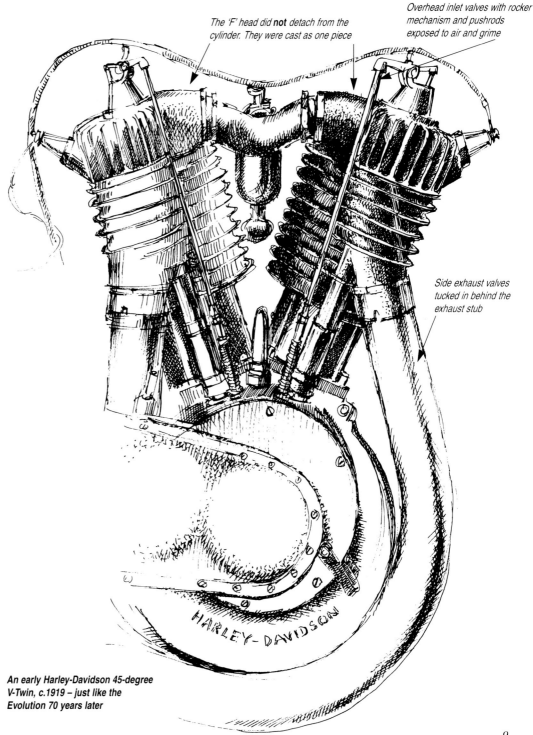

The 'F' head did **not** detach from the cylinder. They were cast as one piece

Overhead inlet valves with rocker mechanism and pushrods exposed to air and grime

Side exhaust valves tucked in behind the exhaust stub

The Harley-Davidson company is of course famous for the production of V-twin-engined motorcycles and the first successful one made by the firm was introduced in 1911. It was soon followed by the 8E, a 45-degree 61-cu in (1000-cc) V-twin of 1912. In the year following, sales of Harley-Davidsons reached a high of 12,904 and the company looked to export markets for the first time engaging an Englishman, Duncan Watson, to arrange imports and sales in the U.K. and Europe. The outbreak of the First World War caused the cessation of exports to Europe less than a year later and were not resumed until 1919. The war did have a positive side for Harley-Davidson as they supplied a number of their motorcycles to the U.S. Army. In the years immediately after the Armistice, exports to Europe were resumed and in 1921

An early Harley-Davidson 45-degree V-Twin, c.1919 – just like the Evolution 70 years later

Douglas Davidson (no relation), aboard a Harley-Davidson, became the first person to exceed 100 mph (161 km/h) on a motorcycle in Britain. He recorded a speed of 100.76 mph at the famous English racing circuit known as Brooklands. The year was not altogether an auspicious one for the company because sales were down more than 18,000 on 1920's record high of 28,189 and for the first time the company made a loss. One of the reasons for this slump in sales was Ford's mass-produced car, the Model T, which at this time was selling for almost the same price as a sidecar outfit. Around this time, approximately 75 per cent of Harley-Davidson's machines left the factory equipped with sidecars. Exports did not suffer as badly and the Harley-Davidson company embarked on a programme to bolster sales around the globe. An employee, Alfred Rich Child, went to Cape Town in South Africa and rode north the full length of the African continent on a J Model. En route he sold 400 motorcycles and established a number of new dealers. After this trip Child went to Japan and spent the next 13 years importing Harley-Davidson motorcycles into the country. He also established a licensing agreement to enable Harleys to be made in Japan by a company called Rikuo. After the 1921 low, sales began to increase again, no doubt aided by the introduction of the first 74-cu in (1200-cc) displacement models. The large capacity of the engine made it more suitable for pulling a sidecar and matched that of major rival Indian Motorcycles of Springfield, Massachusetts. This first 74 was known as an F-head, a descriptive term used to indicate the position of the inlet and exhaust valves. Earlier models were known as IOE – inlet over exhaust.

In 1928 a new chapter opened for Harley-Davidson: not only did it start fitting front brakes to its products for the first time but it unveiled a new engine. It was a side-valve design of V-twin that displaced 45 cu in (740cc). The new model was tagged the Model D. The infamous Wall Street Crash of 1929 dealt manufacturers of most commodities a severe blow, including Harley-Davidson. Its sales declined over the next years to an all-time low of only 3703 machines. Export sales were hit by the introduction of higher import taxes in Australia

Early oil pump used from 1915 to help elimante the problem of over-oiling; a major headache for the total loss system.

Boardtrack racing was a major form of motorcycle sport in the early years of the 20th century and Harley developed V-twin eight-valve racers (opposite top) in order to compete with the likes of Indian, Excelsior, Flying Merkel and Cyclone. The engine (opposite below) was advanced for its day, featuring total loss lubrication and external pushrods (left). The bike featured on these pages was made in 1923.

Pages 12-13
A twenties J Model Harley-Davidson.

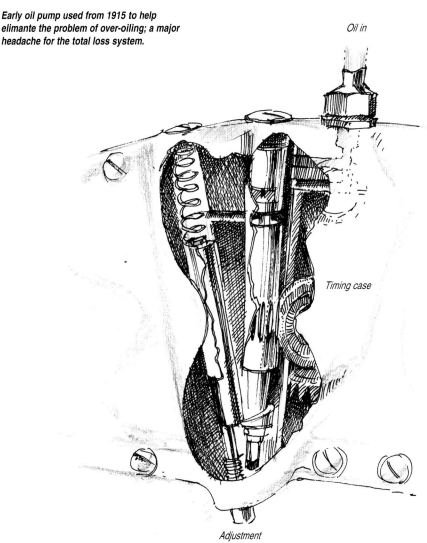

Oil in

Timing case

Adjustment

and New Zealand which must have contributed to this low figure. Another American motorcycle manufacturer, Excelsior, was not able to withstand the pressure and closed in 1931 leaving Indian Motorcycles as Harley-Davidson's only domestic U.S. competitor. Harley-Davidson resorted to desperate measures to attract customers: a choice of colours, extra chrome parts, optional accessories and even an extra wheel were introduced. The Milwaukee company unveiled the Servicar in 1932. This was a three-wheeled machine powered by the 45-cu in sidevalve engine. It was aimed at small businesses, garages and police departments. Garages would send their mechanics out on them to breakdowns, small businesses used them as delivery vehicles, and policemen handed out parking tickets from them. The first Servicars featured the D-model engine although they were later upgraded in line with the solo 45-cu in models. The upgrades included new designations, R and RL models and subsequently WL models. There were also 74- and 80-cu in flatheads designated V and later U Models. Parallel to the development of the sidevalve was that of the company's first overhead valve engine. It created a sensation when it was unveiled in 1936 as the 61-cu in EL model. The style established by the 1936 EL Knucklehead and soon incorporated into both displacements of flathead has endured to this day and is still plainly evident in the design of current models: it is from this starting point that the chapters of this book unfold.

The company became unionized in 1936, further evidence of the uncertain times that bedevilled that decade as the clouds of war gathered in Europe. The United States prepared for war as though it was inevitable that the country would soon become embroiled. Mechanization of the U.S. Army's cavalry units had begun in the late thirties but it was not until 1940 that sufficient funds would be available to procure enough equipment to complete the process. Harley-Davidson sought to supply motorcycles to the Army and shipped some WL models to Fort Knox – more famous as the nation's bullion depository – for evaluation by the Mechanized Cavalry Board. The company (as well as Indian) received small contracts

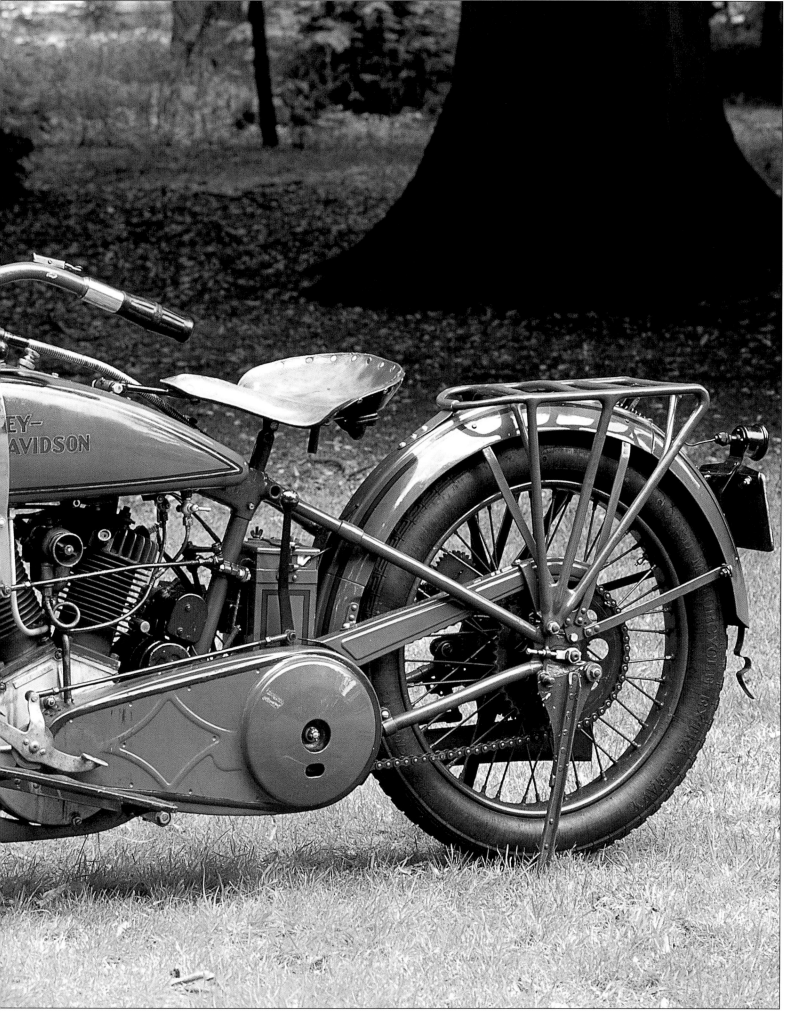

to supply motorcycles; Harley-Davidson supplied the WLA – an Army version of the WL. The Canadian military also ordered motorcycles (Canada had become involved in the Second World War prior to the United States) and a machine tagged the WLC was specifically built for Canada. The WLA and WLC differed only in details. The reorganization of the U.S. Army involved a new divisional structure. Each Division was to consist of three independent infantry regiments and support units with enough transport to move regimental-sized groups. There would also be reconnaissance troops who would ride point at the front of the Division. These soldiers were intended to be mobile and equipped with a variety of trucks and motorcycles; of the latter there were eight solos and three combinations per troop. Unlike the German Army who had machine gun-armed sidecar outfits, the U.S. Army saw the motorcycle as a replacement for the horse, the idea being that the motorcycles would carry the scouts forward from where dismounted scouting could be carried out. This structure was quickly modified as other technology

became available. The Jeep, which was introduced in 1941, was soon relegated to service tasks away from the fighting. They became the workhorses of despatch riders, military policemen and the like and as such stimulated sufficient demand for Harley-Davidson to continue building military motorcycles for the duration of the war. The WLAs and WLCs changed slightly from year to year as refinements were introduced while rubber parts, for example, were reduced due to the short supply of the commodity after numerous Japanese conquests. Harley-Davidson made approximately 88,000 motorcycles during the war years and a large percentage of these were supplied to the other allied nations. The factory received a number of accolades in the form of Army/Navy E for Excellence awards for these efforts. The first of these was awarded on 12 May 1943.

Civilian production resumed after the cessation of hostilities but things only really got back to normal in 1947 when raw materials again became more freely available. Boom years followed: in 1948 the factory sold 31,163 bikes. It was not to last though,

imports from Europe began to flood the U.S. market. Indian could not compete and closed in 1953. Harley-Davidson preferred to compete head-on and introduced motorcycles designed to do exactly that. The K-model was one such machine and a curious mixture of old and new. The last 45-cu in W-series flathead was made in 1951 but a new flathead engine was fitted to the K-model. Harley Davidson upgraded the motorcycle to overhead valves in 1957 and redesignated it the XL: it also became known as the Sportster for the first time. The Sportster name has endured until the present time and the development of this model has paralleled that of the Big Twins.

The big twin-engined Harleys were also sequentially upgraded. The Panhead superseded the Knucklehead in 1948 and was itself superseded by the Shovelhead in 1966. The Shovelhead was to take Harley through the seventies and the years of AMF ownership. By the mid-sixties Harley Davidson's share of the U.S. domestic motorcycle market had contracted considerably and only 3 per cent of its production was being exported. It became clear that Harley – the last American motorcycle manufacturer – would go the way of Indian unless it received a substantial injection of dollars.

There was a certain amount of negotiation before Harley-Davidson was bought by American Machine and Foundry. This group was a huge conglomerate owning a variety of leisure and industrial companies. AMF took control on 7 January 1969. It was not an entirely happy marriage and led to a strike over job losses, quality control problems and all the other symptoms of dissatisfied industry. Despite the problems, the early seventies were boom years for motorcycle sales and the AMF-controlled company upped production enormously. In the long term this was to compound quality control problems but this was not immediately evident. AMF is often criticized during the period of its ownership of Harley-Davidson and the way it ran things but it is now generally accepted that if AMF had not bought Harley-Davidson in 1969 the company would not have survived. The seventies was the era of the new generation of Japanese superbikes and AMF began to consider withdrawing from the Harley-Davidson operation.

Led by Vaughn Beals, who had joined Harley-Davidson in 1975 as Vice-President, a group of 13 Harley-Davidson executives raised $100 million and bought the company from AMF in 1981. The advertising of the time was boosted by evocative lines such as 'The eagle soars alone'. *Easyriders* magazine reported in April 1982 that 'Harley currently sells only 31 per cent of bikes in the over-1000cc market. Honda has a 26 per cent share, Kawasaki has 16 per cent and the other Japanese manufacturers are coming on like Yamamoto at Pearl Harbor'. Vaughn Beals, in an interview designed to discover the reasons why AMF wished to part with Harley-Davidson was quoted as saying: 'Aggression is the key word in this industry, without it you lose your market and AMF had lost the will to fight for Harley-Davidson's share of the market.' According to Beals, AMF, who had already spent vast sums on plant building and modernization after buying Harley-Davidson had decided it was not going to pump any more money into the firm. 'It had to justify Harley-Davidson's expenses against those of its 30 or 40 other

businesses', Beals recalled, 'but those of us who were running AMF's motorcycle products group had to justify what was right for Harley against what was right for AMF. It was a stand off.' He also added that 'AMF considered our offer as a sort of last resort.' It may once have soared alone like an eagle, but it soon flew into troubled skies. Between 1980 and 1982 Harley-Davidson had to lay off a portion of its workforce and the management appealed to the Government to increase tariffs on imported Japanese motorcycles of over 700cc displacement. Harley-Davidson felt that heavyweights from Japan such as the Honda Goldwing were its main threat. The U.S. Government, under the presidency of Ronald Reagan, imposed tariffs of up to 50 per cent on such imports and Reagan himself went as far as visiting one of Harley-Davidson's plants. However, better days were just around the corner for the company and in 1983 another new engine was announced, officially designated the Evolution. The Evolution engine was to be Harley-Davidson's salvation and by 1984 motorcycle magazines were able to report that Harley-Davidson's laid off workers were to be re-employed, its market share had increased and that the company had made a profit for the first time in three years. Vaughn Beals of Harley-Davidson was quoted as saying: 'We're not out of the woods yet but we're working hard to get there. We have an obligation to the American people and the government to take advantage of the breathing room the tariffs provide. We intend to fulfil that obligation by finishing up the job at hand.'

One of the ways the company went about this was by aggressively marketing the new engine – the Evolution – a name that is entirely appropriate: the bottom end of the 80-cubic inch (1340-cc) engine can trace its origins back through the Shovelhead and Panhead to the original 61E Knucklehead of 1936. This engine was the one major factor above all else that saved Harley-Davidson from going out of business and turned it into a major force in the ranks of the world's motorcycle producers. The Evolution engine could conceivably be the final chapter in Harley-Davidson's history of producing air-cooled engines rather than of motorcycle production as a whole. Increasingly, strin-

gent emissions regulations could mean that liquid-cooled engines will power Harleys of the future. This is not a wholly unfounded speculation for in recent years Harley-Davidson has been campaigning a liquid-cooled race bike – the VR1000. It has not been without problems but few developmental machines are and it is common practice to iron out technical problems on the racetrack prior to turning to mass production.

Above
The J Models featured an inlet-over-exhaust valve configuration engine which was produced until the engine type was replaced by the big twin sidevalves in 1930.

Opposite
The J Models had a high level of specification which included either generator of magneto ignition. Lights, sprung forks, tank shifter and cylindrical toolbox were all standard features.

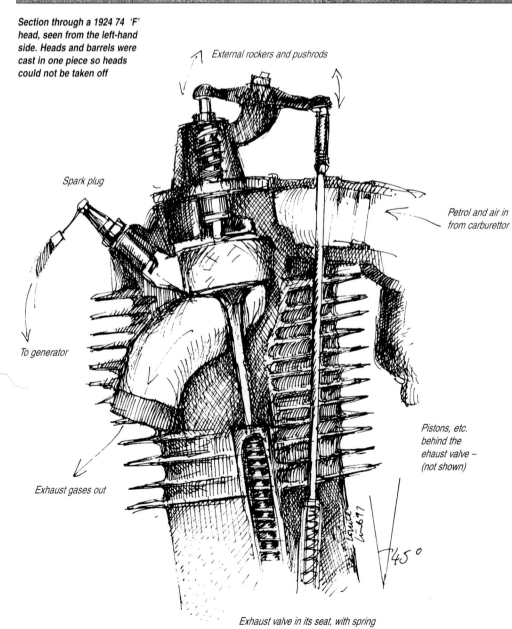

Section through a 1924 74 'F' head, seen from the left-hand side. Heads and barrels were cast in one piece so heads could not be taken off

External rockers and pushrods

Spark plug

Petrol and air in from carburettor

To generator

Pistons, etc. behind the ehaust valve – (not shown)

Exhaust gases out

45°

Exhaust valve in its seat, with spring

Chapter One
THE FLATHEAD

At the time that the first 74-cubic inch (1200-cc) Harleys were introduced in 1921 they featured what is known as F-head valve configuration, where the inlet valve was in the cylinder head while the exhaust valve was in the side of the cylinder head. The larger capacity engine was intended as Harley's competition to the Indian 74 and came in two versions: one featured a magneto and the other a generator, the FD and JD models respectively. By 1928 the JD and the smaller capacity model, the J, were available in performance versions as the JDL and JL and they were also fitted with front brakes for the first time. It was, however, in 1930 that new model Big Twins, designated V, were introduced and these would put Harley-Davidson on the road to the success it has achieved today.

The new Model V 74 cu in (1200cc) was almost entirely new and shared few components with its F-head predecessor. The V models featured a sidevalve engine where both inlet and exhaust valves were positioned alongside the cylinder bore. The cylinder heads, as a result, featured no moving parts and soon earned the nickname of flatheads which soon became the term by which these models were differentiated from other models of the Harley-Davidson reper-

The four-stroke sidevalve V-twin VL engine displaced 74 cubic inches and there were a number of variants during the production run, such as those with higher compression ratios and magneto ignition.

Sidevalve position and action

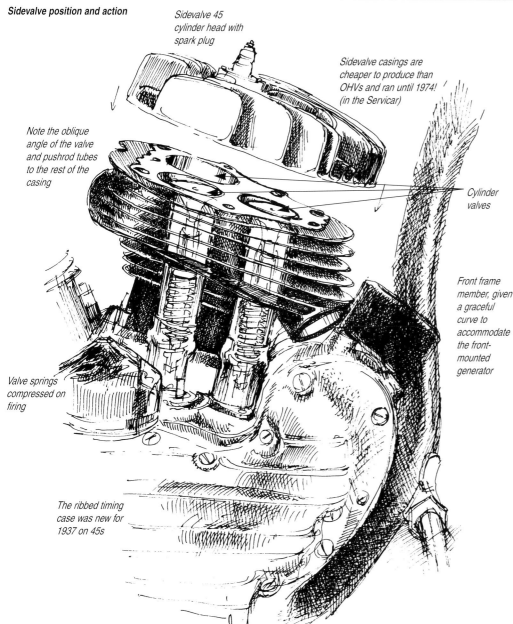

Sidevalve 45 cylinder head with spark plug

Sidevalve casings are cheaper to produce than OHVs and ran until 1974! (in the Servicar)

Note the oblique angle of the valve and pushrod tubes to the rest of the casing

Cylinder valves

Front frame member, given a graceful curve to accommodate the front-mounted generator

Valve springs compressed on firing

The ribbed timing case was new for 1937 on 45s

toire. The cylinder heads were not completely flat; on the top they featured a number of cooling fins cast in during production and on their underside could be found a shaped combustion chamber. Each cylinder head was, of course, drilled and threaded for the spark plug.

The V models featured a total loss lubrication system and were offered for sale in a number of guises, the V and the higher compression VL being two. These were followed by the magneto-equipped VM and VLM as well as machines with varying compression ratios, the VS for sidecar work and the sporting VLD, first mass-produced in 1934. A larger displacement model was also available – the VLH – which displaced 80 cu in (1340cc). The sporting VLD featured a Y-shaped inlet manifold rather than the T-shaped one fitted to the earlier models. Harley-Davidson used carburettors manufactured for it by Linkert and fitted a 1.25-inch M21 item to the VLD which produced 36 bhp. While Harley-Davidson was still manufacturing total loss lubrication engines its competitor, Indian, had advanced to dry sump lubrication: however, Harley would soon up the stakes with both dry sump lubrication and overhead valves in the EL model of 1936, the first Knucklehead.

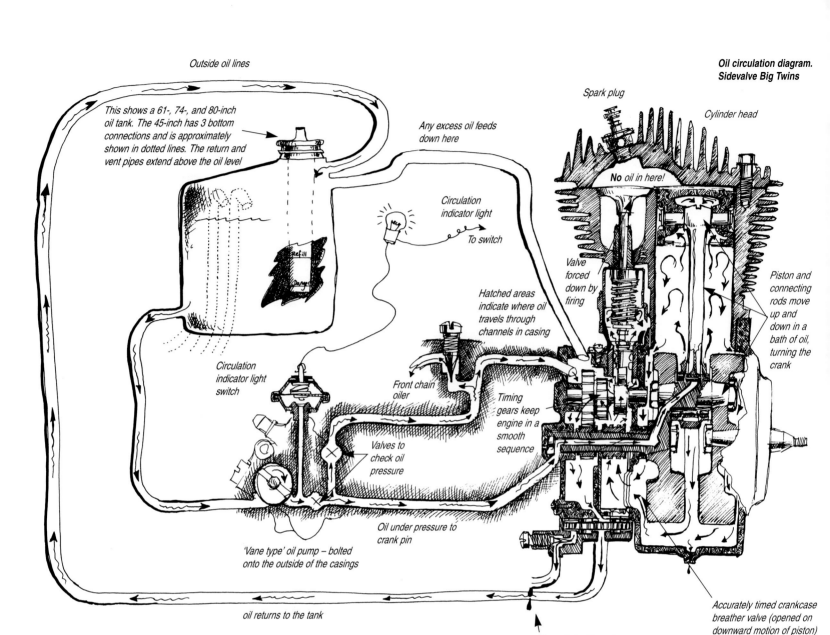

Outside oil lines

This shows a 61-, 74-, and 80-inch oil tank. The 45-inch has 3 bottom connections and is approximately shown in dotted lines. The return and vent pipes extend above the oil level

Any excess oil feeds down here

Spark plug

Cylinder head

No oil in here!

Circulation indicator light

To switch

Valve forced down by firing

Piston and connecting rods move up and down in a bath of oil, turning the crank

Hatched areas indicate where oil travels through channels in casing

Circulation indicator light switch

Front chain oiler

Timing gears keep engine in a smooth sequence

Valves to check oil pressure

Oil under pressure to crank pin

'Vane type' oil pump – bolted onto the outside of the casings

oil returns to the tank

Rear chain oil supply

Accurately timed crankcase breather valve (opened on downward motion of piston)

1930 VL

The V Model series was an almost entirely new motorcycle when it was introduced, sharing few parts with its F-head predecessor. Around 13 variants of the sidevalve V Models were produced through the production run that had variations in specifications, such as those equipped with magnetos and higher compression bikes. The V Series became the U Series in 1937 with the introduction of dry sump lubrication.

As well as producing 74-cu in displacement motorcycles Harley-Davidson produced smaller machines, including the Model D announced in 1928. It failed to get off to the best of starts due to an unreliable gearbox and clutch and was only capable of 55 mph (89 km/h). It was discontinued for 1929 while the problems were resolved and reintroduced in 1930 in three guises, the D, DL and DLD. The different designations referred to the differing power outputs of the

machines; 15, 18.5 and 20 horsepower respectively. The D models featured a vertical generator at the front of the engine which earned them the nickname of the 'three cylinder Harley'. The range of D models became redesignated the R, RL and RLD in 1932 when the generator was repositioned and the pistons were redesigned along with the oil pump, flywheels and clutch.

Despite the introduction of the overhead valve EL models in 1936, the company did not abandon its production of sidevalve big twins. In 1937 the range was redesignated U, UL and ULH as it was upgraded to dry sump lubrication. The smaller capacity V-twins were also changed to dry sump lubrication and redesignated the W, WL and WLD. The WLD was a sports version of the WL but the WL would become famous in its military guise as the WLA and WLC when it was adopted by the armed forces of several allied nations. The A suffix indicates an Army

Technical Specification 1930 VL	
Capacity	73.66 cu in (1207cc)
Engine Cycle	Four stroke
Engine Type	V-twin Flathead
Valve configuration	Sidevalve
Top Speed	85 mph (137 km/h)
Power	n/a
Transmission	Three speed
Frame	Steel loop

Right
The sidevalve engines were significantly upgraded in 1937 and the timing cover seen here was replaced by a ribbed aluminium item.

Below
The 45-cu in displacement Model D made its début in 1928 and was soon followed by the DL, DLD and DS variants. This machine dates from 1930, the twin headlamps being replaced by a single one from the next year.

specification machine while a C suffix indicates a Canadian Army specification. The two models differed only in details and were used all around the world during the war years. In the years afterwards they became popular as cheap civilian transport and popularized Harley-Davidsons in countries where the American machines were not widely available.

The pre-war 750-cc sidevalve-engined motorcycle was militarized and supplied to allied armies during the Second World War. The WLA was supplied to both American and Chinese Armies while the WLC, though originally built for the Canadian forces, was also supplied to Britain, Russia, Australia and South Africa. Harley built in excess of 88,000 machines for the war effort and

Springer forks

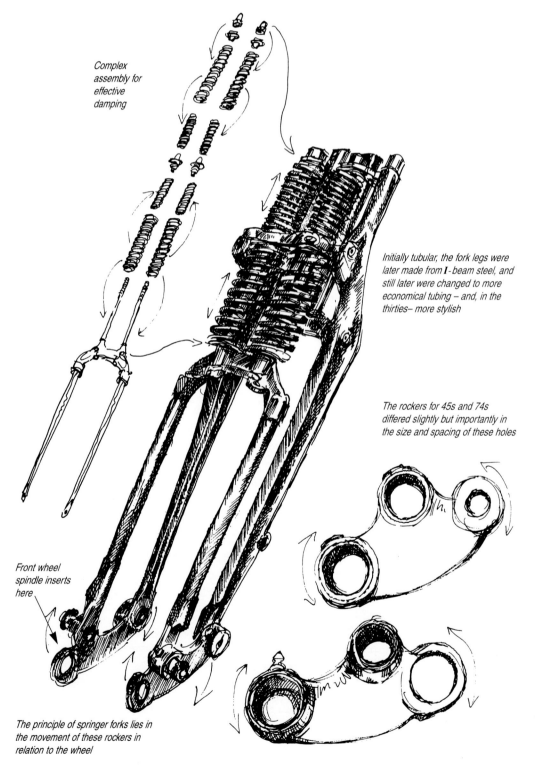

Complex assembly for effective damping

Initially tubular, the fork legs were later made from **I**-beam steel, and still later were changed to more economical tubing – and, in the thirties– more stylish

The rockers for 45s and 74s differed slightly but importantly in the size and spacing of these holes

Front wheel spindle inserts here

The principle of springer forks lies in the movement of these rockers in relation to the wheel

Technical Specification 1942 WLA	
Capacity	45.12 cu in (740cc)
Engine Cycle	Four stroke
Engine Type	V-twin flathead
Valve configuration	Sidevalve
Top Speed	65 mph (105 km/h)
Power	23 bhp @ 4600 rpm
Transmission	Three speed
Frame	Steel loop

earned a special award from the U.S. Army for its achievement.

This was an experimental motorcycle built at the request of the U.S. Government and closely styled on the flat twin German BMW machines in use by the Wehrmacht at the time. Despite its acceptance as a practical motorcycle, the U.S. Army did not order vast numbers for its war effort because by the time it was ready for mass production its

requirement had changed owing to the success of the 4x4 Jeep and the number of WLA and WLC models already produced for America and her allies.

During the war years, Harley-Davidson produced a number of flat twin-engined motorcycles at the request of the U.S. Government and contributed to a number of other military projects. In the years immediately following the Second World War, ex-army Harley-Davidsons were sold to transport hungry civilians around the world. In the United States, new bikes which had not been delivered to the army went on sale while in countries such as Holland Harleys left behind by the Allied Armies were also put up for sale. Many owners, of course, preferred to repaint their old army machines and fit chromed parts and accessories. Some of

Technical Specification – 1924 XA			
Capacity	45.038 cu in (740cc)	Top Speed	n/a
		Power	23 bhp @ 4600 rpm
Engine Cycle	Four stroke		
Engine Type	Flathead twin	Transmission	Four speed
Valve configuration	Sidevalve	Frame	Tubular steel plunger

Flathead 45-cu in Harley Davidsons were produced in large numbers for the allied military during the Second World War including this WLA (above left). The 45s, as they became known, were also produced in civilian trim, as were the larger displacement flatheads (top and above).

The 1948 WL was the civilian version of the military WLA/WLC models that had been widely used during the Second World War. Post-war models such as this (left) featured a number of upgrades such as the hydraulic damper for the springer forks and post-war styling such as the tombstone tail-light and two-light dash. Civilian valanced fenders and chrome trim were also used. They were still powered by the 45-cubic inch displacement sidevalve engine (below).

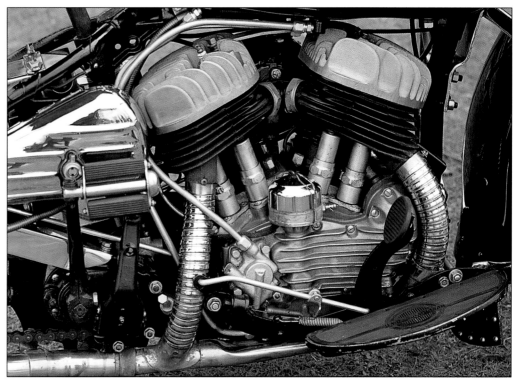

these machines were so well refurbished that it is hard to tell them apart from genuine civilian models, such was the degree of care taken in their renovation. During the post-war years, the 45-cu in flathead models were reintroduced although their styling was upgraded to match the remainder of Harley Davidson's range. After the interruption caused by the Second World War, Harley-Davidson resumed civilian motorcycle production. Shortages of raw materials initially caused difficulties but gradually these were overcome and things got back to normal. Production of the WL resumed in almost the same form as the pre-war models – once again the fenders were valanced and the diameter of the wheels was reduced to 16 inches and chromed parts returned. There were upgrades to the model however; the tail-light and dash covers were redesigned and matched those to be found on other models in the post-war range. The WL was reintroduced, but into a changed world where time was running out for the sidevalve design

of engine as a viable motor in a modern motorcycle: it was only a matter of time before the small-capacity sidevalve was considered obsolete. The flathead solos were discontinued in 1952, although the Sportster would in time take its place. Production of the same 45-cubic inch flathead engine continued as the power plant for the three-wheeled Servicar which remained in production until 1973.

The Servicar was upgraded with the fitment of an electric start in 1964 when its model designation was changed from G to GE. This meant that the humble working Servicar was actually the first Harley-Davidson to come equipped with an electric starter – the mighty Electra Glide did not appear until 1965. The difference between pre- and post-1964 Servicars is easy to spot as the later machines have a large alternator mounted on the frame downtube. The starter itself is mounted on top of the transmission and drives the outer clutch hub to start the engine. The large unit was deemed necessary

to sufficiently charge the battery to ensure enough power for starting. Some other changes to the Servicar were made in conjunction with those made to the solos and others independently. An example of the latter is the shift from spoked wheels to pressed steel ones at the rear and another was the shift from steel load boxes to moulded glass fibre ones.

Above
The 45-cu in RL which carried Harley Davidson through the Depression and was subsequently upgraded and redesignated as the WL.

Top
Another sidevalve 45-cu inch solo motorcycle, seen here in civilian post-war trim. The same engine was used to power the three-wheeled Servicar.

Opposite
From left to right, these are 1942, 1955 and 1937 models.

The Harley 45 established itself in various guises as Harley's racer in American Class C competition.

Above
Al Perry in an AHRMA event on his 1939 WLDD.

Right
A WR engine, the R suffix indicating a racebike.

Above
Class C was introduced by the American Motorcycle Association in the thirties to encourage competition among relative stock bikes which is why this 45 looks remarkably like its roadgoing counterparts with the exception of the fenders which could be removed according to the rules.

Right
The WLDD was the pre-war racer from Harley Davidson intended to compete with Indian's Sport Scout.

Chapter Two
THE KNUCKLEHEAD

Parallel to the development of the sidevalve engine, the Milwaukee factory was developing an overhead valve design and the engine went into production in 1936. It was designated the 61E Model, the 61 referring to its displacement in cubic inches (1000cc). The engine came to be known as the 'Knucklehead' because its rocker covers bore some resemblance to knuckles. The Knucklehead was the first Harley to have dry sump lubrication – oil recirculating between the oil tank and engine – instead of a total loss system. The oil tank, horseshoe-shaped, was located under the seat, the engine was fitted into a double loop frame and a new style of gas tank appeared. It was made in two halves, hid the frame tubes, and had the speedo set into a dash plate that fitted between the two halves of the tank.

The EL model was soon in the news when Joe Petrali rode one to achieve various speed records on the sands of Daytona Beach in Florida. Despite its advanced engine, much of the remainder of the machine was typical of Harley-Davidsons of the time. The frame was of the rigid type with no rear suspension, rider comfort was provided by means of a sprung saddle and the forks were still of the springer design. The outbreak of the Second World War in Europe did not affect the production of civilian motorcycles for the U.S. domestic market; but the Japanese airstrike of December 1941 against Pearl Harbor in Hawaii did. Civilian motorcycle production was suspended almost immediately as industrial companies, such as Harley-

Left
The engine that became universally known as the Knucklehead was introduced in 1936 as the 61-cu in displacement EL model. Production was interrupted by the Second World War and the engine was superseded by the Panhead in 1948.

Right
Over the years Harley-Davidson produced a variety of faces for tank-mounted speedometers for both civilian and military uses as well as 'police specials'.

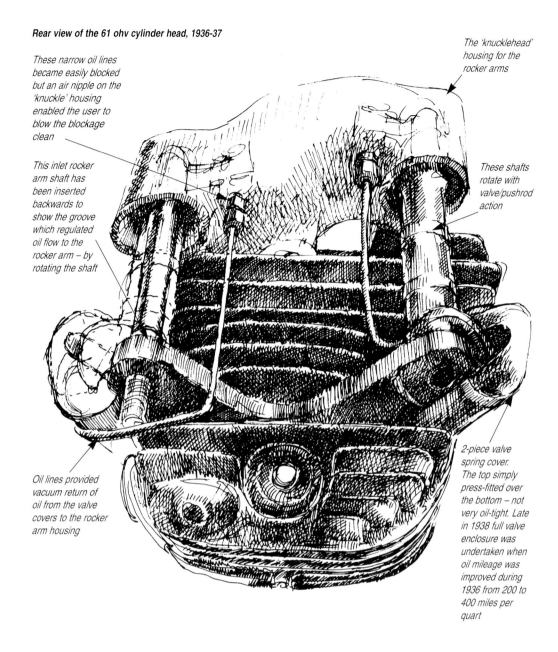

Rear view of the 61 ohv cylinder head, 1936-37

These narrow oil lines became easily blocked but an air nipple on the 'knuckle' housing enabled the user to blow the blockage clean

This inlet rocker arm shaft has been inserted backwards to show the groove which regulated oil flow to the rocker arm – by rotating the shaft

The 'knucklehead' housing for the rocker arms

These shafts rotate with valve/pushrod action

Oil lines provided vacuum return of oil from the valve covers to the rocker arm housing

2-piece valve spring cover. The top simply press-fitted over the bottom – not very oil-tight. Late in 1938 full valve enclosure was undertaken when oil mileage was improved during 1936 from 200 to 400 miles per quart

Davidson, turned their production lines over to the war effort. The military specification WLs were produced in large numbers along with a tiny number of other models for police and 'essential use' purposes. Knucklehead production resumed in the immediate post-war years but the technology had been refined and much had been learned during the conflict which meant that another new overhead valve Harley Davidson big twin would soon make its appearance. It arrived to critical acclaim in 1948 and was quickly referred to as the Panhead.

At the end of the Second World War, companies such as Harley-Davidson resumed civilian production. Harley initially reintroduced the motorcycles from its pre-war range to satisfy the eager demand from returning servicemen for new motorcycles, while it prepared new and updated models. The 1947 Knucklehead was one of the pre-war machines reintroduced and almost the last of the EL and FL Knuckleheads. It was to be superseded the following year by the Panhead, albeit in a similar frame and cycle parts. The Knucklehead was available as a 61-cu in (1000cc) machine from 1936, designated the 61E, and as a 74-cu in (1200cc) – the 61F – from 1941. Production of both models was suspended in the latter year, after Pearl Harbor. It is generally accepted that the 61E was the first of the modern Harleys with dry sump lubrication and the one from which all current Harleys draw their styling.

Close scrutiny of the pre- and post-war Knuckleheads reveal a number of styling changes that were made for the 1947 model year. Between 1936 and 1946, Harley-Davidson had fitted a rounded tail-light to its machines: it was superseded for the 1947 bikes with a new design. In the same way that Harley parts acquire nicknames to differentiate one from another, two different tail-lights soon came to be referred to as the bee-hive and tombstone respectively. The shapes of the two electrical components bear a distinct resemblance to the objects for which they are named. Other changes, at the same time, included a shift from the cat's eye dash cover to a more modern-looking one, now known as the two-light dash because, much later, it in turn was superseded by another dash. The cat's eye and two-light designations refer to the type of ignition and oil

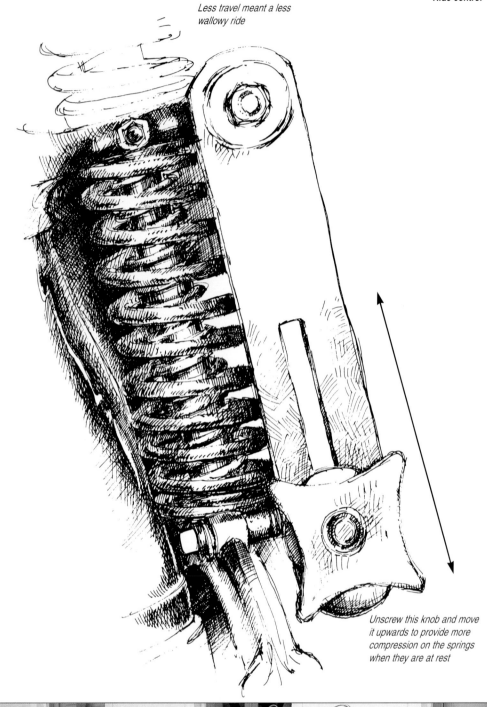

Less travel meant a less wallowy ride

Unscrew this knob and move it upwards to provide more compression on the springs when they are at rest

Linkert carburettors such as these were used by Harley-Davidson on many of its V-twins, including Knuckleheads such as this one (right) where it fits onto the inlet manifold between the cylinders and is concealed behind the circular air cleaner.

Opposite below
A restored pre-war Knucklehead – saddlebags and fringed solo saddle are typical of the era. Springer forks, valanced fenders and fatbob tanks were factory stock items.

Technical Specification
1936 EL

Capacity	60.33 cu in (988.56 CC)
Engine Cycle	Four stroke
Engine Type	V-twin Knucklehead
Valve configuration	Overhead valve
Top Speed	90 mph (145 km/h)
Power	40 bhp
Transmission	Four speed
Frame	Double loop

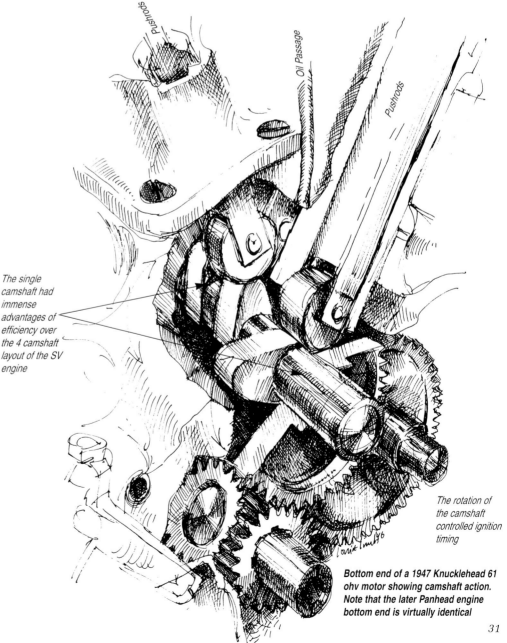

Pushrods

Oil Passage

Pushrods

The single camshaft had immense advantages of efficiency over the 4 camshaft layout of the SV engine

The rotation of the camshaft controlled ignition timing

Bottom end of a 1947 Knucklehead 61 ohv motor showing camshaft action. Note that the later Panhead engine bottom end is virtually identical

warning lights used adjacent to the speedometer. Front fender lights were changed and in place of the manually adjusted ride control was fitted a hydraulic damper.

The Knucklehead was the first Harley-Davidson overhead valve V-twin and featured dry sump lubrication where the oil circulated between a tank and the engine instead of the earlier total loss systems. This motorcycle set the style for Harley-Davidsons which still endures, with its rounded two-piece gas tank in which the speedo and dash are mounted.

A variety of post-war Knuckleheads including (top left) Stuart Hall's 1947 model. The Knucklehead was reintroduced, essentially in its pre-war form, after the end of the Second World War. Major components such as the engine, transmission, frame, fenders and forks were unchanged although a number of smaller components were redesigned, including tail-lights and tank-mounted dashes.

Opposite
It is possible to tell at a glance whether a Knucklehead is pre- or post-war by looking at the tail-lights. This bike has a 'beehive' tail-light, used by Harley-Davidson between 1936 and 1946, while the German-registered machine (inset) has a 'tombstone' tail-light used by Harley-Davidson between 1947 and 1954. The method is not guaranteed on modified Harleys because both types of tail-light are popular with customizers.

Below
The 'cat's eye' dash – so called because of the shape of the oil and ignition warning lights – was used by Harley-Davidson between 1936 and 1946.

Right
The 'two-light' dash was used between 1947 and 1954. The two-light dash is so described to differentiate it from the later three-light dash. It aids accurate dating of a Harley but, like the tail-lights, both types are popular with customizers.

Chapter Three
THE PANHEAD

The Panhead superseded the Knuckle-head models but retained the E and F designations for the 61- and 74-cu in models. The Panhead was essentially a new top end on the existing Knucklehead bottom end and, as the slang name implies, its rocker covers look rather like upturned cooking pans. The cylinder heads were cast from aluminium after problems with the all-iron Knucklehead; hydraulic lifters contributed to a quieter-running engine and a larger oil pump was used to improve lubrication. The improvements would not end there though; the cycle parts of the motorcycle would also be upgraded. Harley-Davidson marketed a Panhead-engined motorcycle for one year only which featured a rigid frame and springer forks. Because of this short period of production these 'Springer Pans' are desirable motorcycles.

The springer forks were replaced by hydraulic telescopic units in 1949 and the big twin was renamed the Hydra-Glide. The

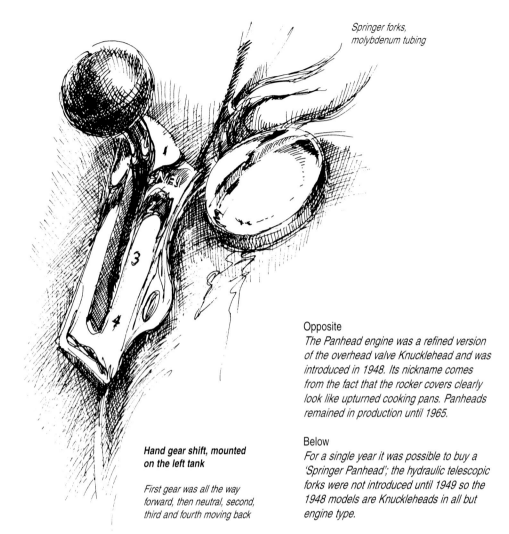

Springer forks, molybdenum tubing

Hand gear shift, mounted on the left tank

First gear was all the way forward, then neutral, second, third and fourth moving back

Opposite
The Panhead engine was a refined version of the overhead valve Knucklehead and was introduced in 1948. Its nickname comes from the fact that the rocker covers clearly look like upturned cooking pans. Panheads remained in production until 1965.

Below
For a single year it was possible to buy a 'Springer Panhead'; the hydraulic telescopic forks were not introduced until 1949 so the 1948 models are Knuckleheads in all but engine type.

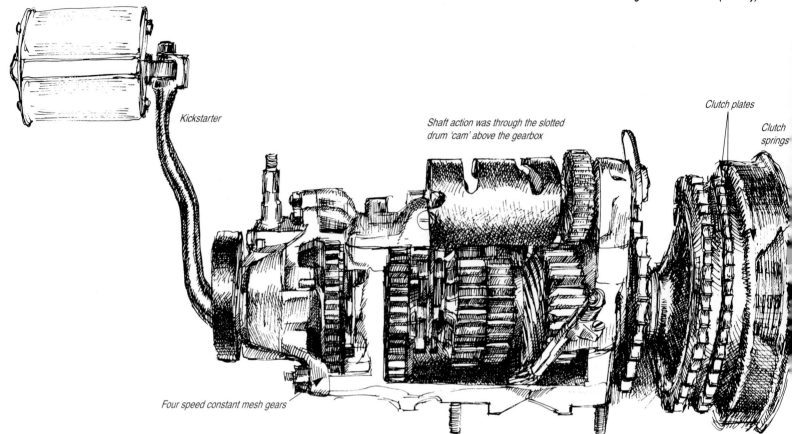

Kickstarter

Shaft action was through the slotted drum 'cam' above the gearbox

Clutch plates

Clutch springs

Four speed constant mesh gears

telescopic front end obviated the need for the hydraulic damper but the remainder of the styling changes introduced for 1947 remained current; tombstone tail-lights and similar are all to be found on early Panheads. In many ways the Hydra-Glide was the crossover between the vintage-style Harleys and those perceived as being more modern. Whereas the springer forks looked vintage because of their exposed and spindly springs, the Hydra-Glide was much more modern with larger diameter telescopic fork legs and a cast headlamp nacelle. The sprung solo and buddy seats were still used according to customer preference in place of rear suspension but Harley's engineers were working on that as the next major update. There were numerous smaller upgrades to the Hydra-Glide before that, however; in 1952 a customer-specified option of a foot gearshift was made available. Panheads so equipped were designated FLF while the traditional handshift remained as the FL. The basic E and F models were discontinued in 1952 and the smaller-capacity EL, ELF and ES in 1953: from then on, Panheads were 74-cu inch only. Details were redesigned, such as the change in 1955 to the three-light dash which featured an extra warning light over the two of earlier models. The three lights were circular, located in different positions to the two rectangular lights used from 1947 to

The Duo Glide featured rear
shock absorption as well as front
telescopic forks

The angle of the shock
absorbers fitted more to the
line of the saddlbags rather
than for effective functioning

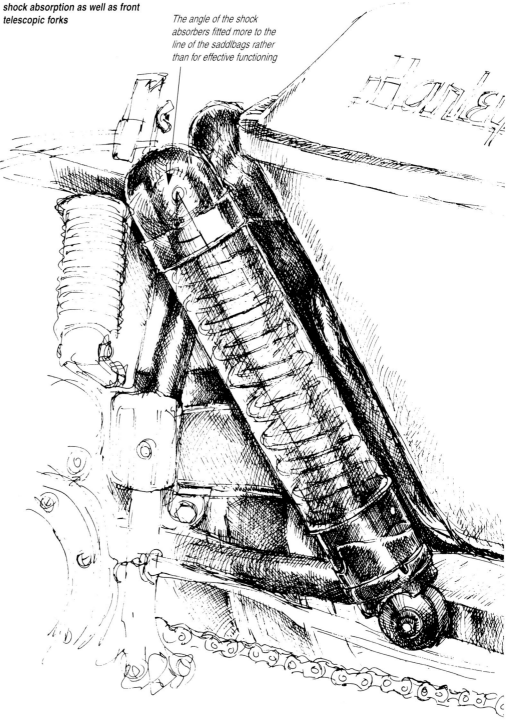

1955. The top of the range big twin for 1955 was the FLH with the stronger bottom end and higher compression. It was the FLH that coined the term 'dresser' as owners of big twins began to accessorize their machines with saddlebags and windshields. Initially, these were made from leather and canvas but as time went by they were manufactured from glass fibre and plastic so that the big bikes which looked even bigger with the accessories came to be described as 'dressed'. Harley-Davidson, who has always marketed a line of official accessories began to offer such

Top left

Various American police departments used Hydra-Glides. They were basic models but fitted with special police equipment, such as a radio and siren.

Left

The progression from Hydra-Glide to Duo Glide is clearly illustrated in this photo from Severance, Colorado. The Hydra-Glide with its rigid frame is on the right while the Duo Glide with a swinging arm and shock absorbers is on the left.

equipment from the showroom floor. The rigid frame was finally upgraded to swing-arm rear suspension in the Duo Glide in 1958.

The name Duo Glide came about because the new models had a 'glide' at both ends, hence Duo, and Harley trumpeted this feature by renaming the big twin models, although there were still FL and FLH models. They were renamed again when the electric start, which appeared in 1965, saw the big twin renamed the Electra-Glide (the hyphen in the name was later dropped), i.e., it was a Duo Glide with electric start.

Alongside these improvements and modifications to the frame and forks of the big twin-powered motorcycles, there were many detail improvements to the engine itself and in all there were six different Panhead engines. The first was made between 1948 and 1953 in both 61- and 74-cu inch capacities, the second type with a different pinion shaft being made only in 1954. The bearings on the engine sprocket shaft were altered for 1955 when a spring-loaded shock-absorbing sprocket was incorporated, and the lubrication system was changed slightly. The next change came for 1958 when the pinion shaft was altered in order to accept larger main bearings and this was how the motor stayed until 1963. In that year the oil feed to the cylinder heads was taken through an external oil line. The final changes were made to the cases and covers of the Panhead to make it suitable for the fitment of the electric starter.

It was around this time that the chopper surfaced as an up-and-coming fashion craze: some Harley riders were accessorizing their bikes in order to dress them up while others, possibly as a reaction, effectively undressed their's by 'chopping' everything off. These bikes bore a strong resemblance to the race-style bobbers of an earlier era, at least for a while, but later developed fashionable features all their own, including over-length forks, small tanks from scooters and mopeds, jockey shift gearchanges and numerous other details. So important did these unofficial styles become to Harley riders around the United States that later, in the Shovelhead era, Harley-Davidson would start to offer mildly customized models out of dealers' showrooms and invent the concept of the 'factory custom'.

Opposite above
The 1965 Electra Glide was a further development of the Duo Glide. As well as suspension front and rear, it featured an electric starter although the kick start was retained.

Left
The first Electra Glides used Panhead engines (above) although they were modified to incorporate the starter mechanism and a larger battery was fitted. The Panhead-engined Electra Glides were soon superseded by those fitted with the Shovelhead engine introduced in 1966.

Harley Davidson introduced its Panhead engine in 1948. It was the successor to the overhead valve Knucklehead and it also had overhead valves. The new engine was originally fitted to Harley's springer fork-equipped rigid frame rolling chassis but this later benefited from hydraulic telescopic forks and so came to be designated the Hydra-Glide. Later, when a swing-arm frame was used to give the Panhead front and rear suspension it was redesignated the Duo Glide, to indicate two suspension systems and later again, in 1965, when an electric starter became available the bike was redesignated the Electra Glide.

The Panhead rocker covers 1948-65

The pan-shaped covers had felt linings designed to soak up excess oil, drip it down into the workings and so reduce noise. Sometimes they fell off causing extra noise and oil leaks.

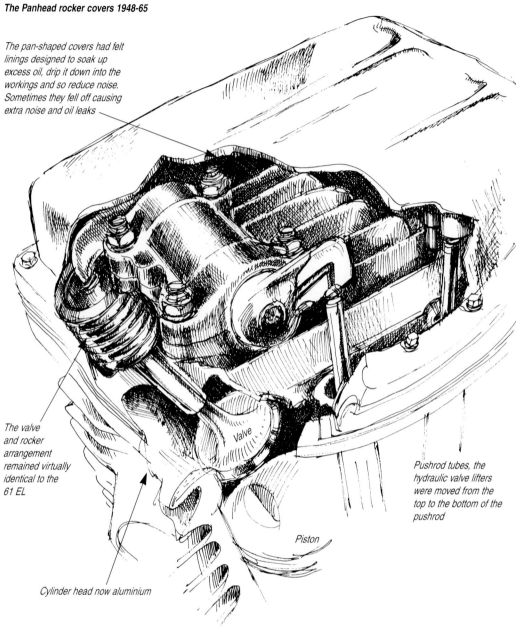

The valve and rocker arrangement remained virtually identical to the 61 EL

Valve

Pushrod tubes, the hydraulic valve lifters were moved from the top to the bottom of the pushrod

Piston

Cylinder head now aluminium

Technical Specification 1949 FL HYDRA-GLIDE	
Capacity	74 cu in (1200cc)
Engine Cycle	Four stroke
Engine Type	V-twin Panhead
Valve configuration	Overhead valve
Top Speed	102 mph (164 km/h)
Power	55 bhp
Transmission	Four speed
Frame	Tubular steel

By 1965 the factory was also fitting glass fibre saddlebags (left) to its motorcycles rather than the ornately decorated leather ones used throughout the forties and fifties and seen on the Hydra-Glide above.

Opposite below
The 1965 Electra Glide was one of the Big Twin Harleys fitted with the 'three-light' dash which was used by the company between 1955 and 1967.

Chapter Four
THE SHOVELHEAD

The Panhead engine was superseded by the Shovelhead in 1966 and, once again, it was a new top end on an existing bottom end. The new engine became known as the Shovelhead because the rocker covers resembled the backs of upturned shovels. Most of the models had designations beginning FL; there were bikes such as the FLB, FLHB and so on. The B suffix denoted electric start and was used until 1969. It was dropped for 1970, presumably because the backup kick starter had been discontinued. The Shovelhead engine as introduced in 1966 was a new type of top end on the latest style Panhead lower end. The new engine featured the same bore and stroke as all big twins back as far as 1941 but not all the parts of these engines were interchangeable. Some other components such as the dash panel and lights were redesigned in 1966, although the idea of a tank-mounted speedo and ignition switch remained. The tombstone tail-light disappeared in favour of a rectangular unit.

The major change to the Shovelhead engine came in 1970 when Harley-Davidson switched from using a D.C. generator to an A.C. alternator. This change required major changes to the crankcases and a number of subtle changes to other parts. As a result of this redesign, early Shovelheads are often referred to as Generator Shovels while later ones are known as Alternators. The way models were numbered changed at this time, too; letters and numbers were substituted for models and years. The Shovelhead was refined almost continuously; for example, between 1966 and 1980, five different oil pumps were used within the engines and they are not all interchangeable.

Of all the models ever produced by Harley-Davidson, it is the mighty Electra Glide that is the most recognizable and the one most worthy of being regarded as an American icon. The Electra Glide was used by many police departments around the United States and beyond and was immortalized in the film *Electra Glide in Blue*. The model designated Electra Glide has had a long production run, from its introduction in

Opposite
The Shovelhead engine was introduced in 1966. It was basically a new top end on a late Panhead bottom end. The nickname is based on the premise that the rocker covers resemble the backs of upturned shovels.

Above
The Shovelhead was made for four years with a generator before being upgraded to an alternator.

1965 to the present day. During this time, no less than three different Harley-Davidson engines have been used to power the biggest Harleys. The seventies models were built under the auspices of the conglomerate, AMF, which owned a glass fibre plant, so fairings, saddlebags and top boxes were made from this material and the large saddle is designed for two people. Progressively, Harley's Big Twins gained weight and size, especially where the FLH models were fitted with hard glass fibre bags. This style of dresser was not to every rider's taste and, in a changing world, a rethink was long overdue.

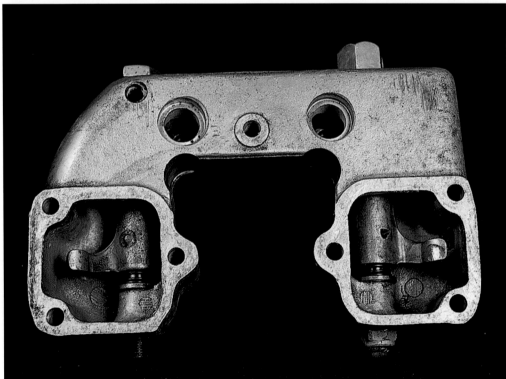

Willie G. Davidson, grandson of one of the company's founders, was employed within Harley's design department and began to consider the possibilities of a new Big Twin which would sit in the company's range between the Electra Glides and the smaller Sportsters. The new Harley-Davidson emerged in 1971, designated the FX Super Glide. This was an Alternator Shovelhead with the slimmer Sportster front end and none of the big dresser's glass fibre bags or fairings. The first models featured an unusually shaped dual seat and tailpiece manufactured in glass fibre but it was discontinued for the second year of production when the Super Glide appeared with a scalloped dual seat, and XL-style rear fender. In many ways it was the first factory custom and also an attempt to compete with the unauthorized, unofficial chopper builders who were thriving, chopping the dresser-style machines. Later, there was a succession of FX models, each designated for a particular detail such as electric start or disc brakes; FXE, FXWG, FXDG, FXR, FXEF and FXB. The Super Glide (FXE) was followed in 1977 by the Low Rider (FXS) which was another factory custom. With its distinctly chopper-style looks; forward control foot pegs, a low seat height and a raked out telescopic front end, it was poles apart from the full dress Electra Glide (FLH). It was instantly popular and Harley Davidson followed it with the Wide Glide (FXWG) and Fat Bob (FXEF) which took the factory custom Harley further along the road towards factory choppers. It featured a longer raked front end in which the fork legs were more widely spaced, a stepped seat and back rest but, most telling of all, a flame paint job on the tank. Such machines were seen as Harley-Davidson's recognition of the needs and aspirations of its customers. Prior to this it had tended to disassociate itself from the chopper-riding bikers. This did it little good as there was resentment from other riders who rightly felt they alone had stuck with Harley when its market share began to drastically contract. Another special Shovelhead was the Sturgis (FXB): it appeared in 1980, named after one of America's huge annual biker gatherings. The Sturgis was a belt drive Shovelhead, painted almost all-black with orange detailing.

The FXR was something of an FLT Tour

Glide, stripped of its touring paraphernalia and an upgraded FXE at the same time. At a glance, the most obvious difference was the appearance of triangulated frame tubes behind the gearbox. The engine used was the rubber mount Shovelhead from the FLT along with a five-speed transmission, the FX/XL style front end and dual shock-absorber swinging-arm rear suspension. It took a new frame to make these components work together and give some cohesion to its appearance. Initially, it was known as Super Glide II, but this disappeared in only 12 months and the FXR designations appeared. The motorcycle was an FX with a rubber mount engine – hence the R suffix. The FXR was fitted with wire wheels and finished with a single colour paint scheme. The FXRS was similar apart from having a pair of cast alloy spoked wheels, highway pegs, sissy bar and a two-tone paint job.

1971 FX Super Glide

The Super Glide was an early factory custom from Harley Davidson, combining as it did the lighter Sportster front end with the brawn of the big twin Shovelhead engine. It was designed by Willie G. Davidson, the grandson of one of the founders, and was seen at the time as a watershed in U.S. motorcycling.

The name Electra Glide lost its hyphen down the years and gained weight as it became equipped with larger saddlebags and fairings, usually made from glass fibre because of AMF's part ownership of a plant which manufactured this material. The motorcycle in this form became famous to many as *the* Harley Davidson and was immortalized on film in *Electra Glide in Blue*. From 1966 to 1979 it was powered by the Shovelhead engine and after 1984 was to be powered by the Evolution Engine.

The Shovelhead V-twin engine powered one of the first factory custom bikes from Harley-Davidson in 1981. The FXWG was available with a customized 'flame' paint scheme similar to that already in vogue with custom builders and painters of the time.

The Electra Glide remained in production alongside the new Super Glide although it was progressively upgraded, being fitted with disc brakes, dual seat and heavyweight touring paraphernalia.

Technical Specification
1971 FX SUPER GLIDE

Capacity	74 cu in (1200cc)
Engine Cycle	Four stroke
Engine Type	V-twin Shovelhead
Valve configuration	Overhead valve
Top Speed	116 mph (187 km/h)
Power	n/a
Transmission	Four speed
Frame	Tubular steel

Above
The AMF-era Big Twins featured a mixture of traditional and modern styling touches.

Left
The dash remained tank-mounted and headlamps remained mounted in a nacelle reminiscent of the Hydra-Glide.

Top far right
The fenders on the Big Twins remained large and fully valanced.

Above far right and right
Disc brakes were introduced. The same brake caliper was used on the Cessna aircraft.

Technical Specification
1979 FLH ELECTRA GLIDE

Capacity	74 cu in (1200 cc)
Engine Cycle	Four stroke
Engine Type	V-twin Shovelhead
Valve configuration	Overhead valve
Top Speed	105 mph (170 km/h)
Power	66 bhp @ 5200 rpm
Transmission	Four speed
Frame	Tubular steel

Technical Specification
1981 FXWG WIDE GLIDE

Capacity	80 cu in (1340 cc)
Engine Cycle	Four stroke
Engine Type	V-twin Shovelhead
Valve configuration	Overhead valve
Top Speed	103 mph (165 km/h)
Power	49 bhp @ 5800 rpm
Transmission	Four speed
Frame	Duplex Tubular steel

Right
A mildly modified 1976 FLH owned by Dale Richardson of Greeley, Colorado. It is typical of many Harleys of this era in that the bike has been modified to the owner's taste so that it remains a practical bike for the nineties. It has been repainted, has earlier tank badges from a 1965 model and features extra chromed parts and a number of other modifications.

Pages 54 and 55
The Evolution engine is appropriately named, simply because it is clearly an evolution of the Knucklehead of 1936. It followed Harley's pattern of gradual sequential upgrades. This time it was an improved top end on an Alternator Shovelhead bottom end along with a number of other improvements.

The Evolution engine was nicknamed Blockhead but the abbreviation 'Evo' is more widely used. The engine itself has to conform to ever more stringent laws regarding noise and exhaust emissions.

Chapter Five
THE EVOLUTION

The Evolution engine was in many ways a much improved 80-cubic inch (1340-cc) Shovelhead engine, a new top end on the Alternator Shovel. It soon gained the nickname Blockhead, continuing in the tradition of describing its rocker covers, but gradually it came to be known as the 'Evo'. It uses alloy cylinder barrels with iron liners and heads which permit greater and more even heat dissipation than the iron and alloy combination of the Shovelhead. The valves were redesigned to allow better flow on both the induction and exhaust strokes of the four-stroke cycle and the combustion chambers were redesigned to meet emissions regulations and be suitable for unleaded gas: the redesign allowed higher compression with lower octane fuel. Also improved were levels of quality control, oil consumption and frequency of maintenance. The engine has become notable for its reliability, gas-mileage and lightness, in short, for being a good engine. The entire range of Big Twins benefited from the new engine and the range was extended with the introduction of the new model, the Softail in 1984.

The FLHTC of 1984 incorporated the new rubber engine mount frame, five-speed transmission and Tour Glide front end partially concealed behind a fairing. Final drive was by means of a chain and engine. In other respects, the machine was the same as the Shovelhead-powered Tour Glide. The new machine was tested by American motorcycle magazines resulting in critical acclaim. The engine was referred to as the V2 by Harley-Davidson and by 1985 had a five-speed belt final drive in the FL models. For the remainder of the eighties the range was subtly altered as improvements were incorporated, one of the few most obvious being the change to a circular air cleaner.

For a year or two there were rigid mount V2-powered swing-arm-framed Super Glides, including Fat Bob, Low Rider and Wide Glide, but the Softail frame was about to change all that. The new Softail models were essentially Super Glides based around a specific new type of frame and had the appear-

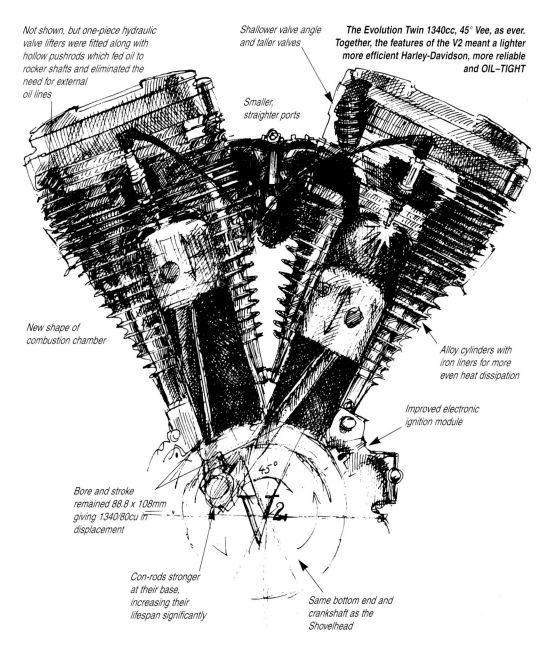

Not shown, but one-piece hydraulic valve lifters were fitted along with hollow pushrods which fed oil to rocker shafts and eliminated the need for external oil lines

Shallower valve angle and taller valves

The Evolution Twin 1340cc, 45° Vee, as ever. Together, the features of the V2 meant a lighter more efficient Harley-Davidson, more reliable and OIL-TIGHT

Smaller, straighter ports

New shape of combustion chamber

Alloy cylinders with iron liners for more even heat dissipation

Improved electronic ignition module

Bore and stroke remained 88.8 x 108mm giving 1340/80cu in displacement

Con-rods stronger at their base, increasing their lifespan significantly

Same bottom end and crankshaft as the Shovelhead

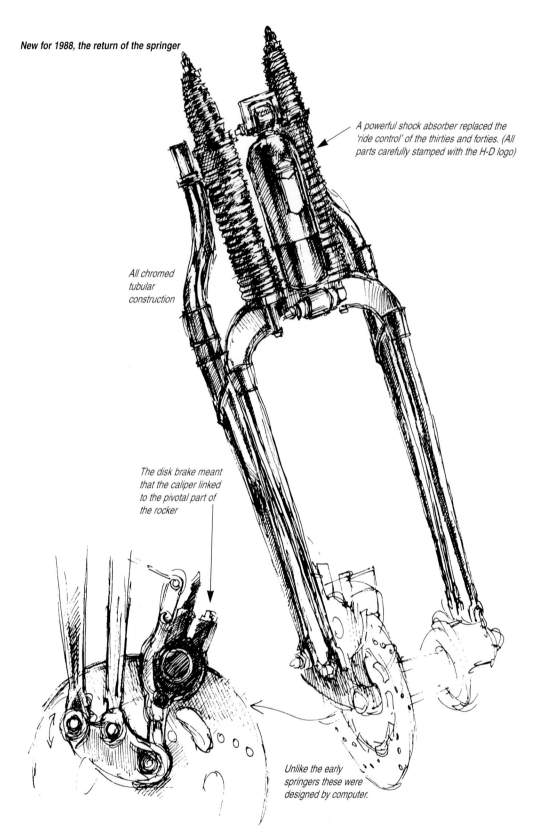

New for 1988, the return of the springer

A powerful shock absorber replaced the 'ride control' of the thirties and forties. (All parts carefully stamped with the H-D logo)

All chromed tubular construction

The disk brake meant that the caliper linked to the pivotal part of the rocker

Unlike the early springers these were designed by computer.

ance of a vintage rigid frame but featured suspension. The shock absorbers were positioned horizontally below the gearbox between the bottom frame rails. The pivot for the suspension was mounted in the rear section of the frame behind the gearbox. The classic look, inspiring feelings of nostalgia, received another boost with the introduction of the Softail Springer in 1988 and the Softail Custom. In 1988, Harley-Davidson astounded the motorcycling world by reintroducing

springer forks which most people assumed had been consigned to the history books, having been completely superseded by telescopic forks. Harley-Davidson had by then begun to market a significant percentage of its motorcycles with a nod to the past. As a result, the reintroduction of components that had last been seen in 1948 became a viable idea. The springer-forked motorcycles have now been in production for eight years and the old-style forks are used on more than one

model. The Bad Boy, which is the nearest thing to a factory-built chopper, is one of the models to use springers. The springer forks used on Evos are a modernized version of the originals designed decades before by William Harley: they have been updated from those used on Knuckleheads and Panheads and are now made with the assistance of computer-aided design and modern materials as well as being fitted with a single disc brake.

Nostalgia and heritage were the selling points for the new Harleys that looked like old Harleys. One such was the 1988 FLST Heritage Softail Classic which was very much a fifties-inspired design of a Harley-Davidson big twin motorcycle redesigned for modern roads and traffic conditions and designed to sell in the rapidly growing nostalgia market. It featured the Softail frame, which was a Harley-Davidson-designed frame that looked like a traditional rigid frame but featured rear suspension to increase the rider and passenger's comfort. The way this was done was to add a pivoted triangulated rear section to the frame in place of the more usual swinging arm. The shock absorber for the new design of frame was hidden underneath. This kept the triangular lines of the frame clearly visible and were not unlike pre-1958 Harley frames. The remainder of the bike was styled in an old way too, big valanced FL fenders, studded saddlebags and saddle and an old-fashioned two-tone paint scheme.

Another such Harley, the Heritage Nostalgia, went on sale in August 1992 and Heritage models have stayed in Harley's range ever since. The FLSTN of 1996 is another contemporary classic Harley-Davidson, based around the Softail frame and Evolution big twin engine. While it looks to the past for such items as partially shrouded telescopic forks and 16-inch whitewall tyres, back and front, it does not have the old-fashioned dresser look of the Heritage Softail Classic but is nonetheless reminiscent of an

Right
Harley Davidson discontinued the use of its distinctive springer forks in 1948 and, after a 40-year gap, reintroduced them. Such was the feeling of nostalgia that the springer Softails produced by Milwaukee were an immediate success. The new springer forks were machined to finer tolerances through the use of CAD and modern machining techniques and featured disc brakes. Nonetheless, they still had that vintage look.

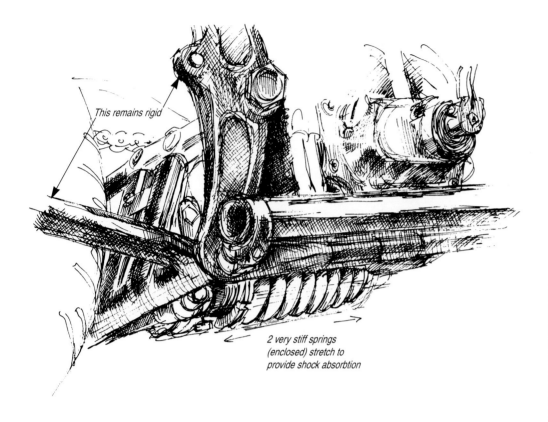

This remains rigid

2 very stiff springs
(enclosed) stretch to
provide shock absorbtion

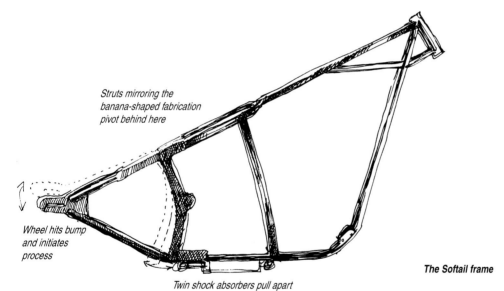

Struts mirroring the
banana-shaped fabrication
pivot behind here

Wheel hits bump
and initiates
process

Twin shock absorbers pull apart

The Softail frame

Below
Harley-Davidson makes its motorcycles appear much older than they actually are through the use of the Softail frame. It is named to differentiate it from the Hardtail, but appears similar. The suspension is hidden and the frame is designed to look like an old rigid frame so that the motorcycle on the right resembles a 1949 Hydra-Glide although it was made 40 years later.

early fifties Hydra-Glide, albeit a slightly customized one. The lines of the FL fenders are unmistakable and the Softail frame gives a rigid frame appearance: it takes more than a glance to spot the pivot for the rear portion of the frame (it is actually between the exhaust pipes behind the gearbox). The chromed oil tank and other components and two-tone paint give the custom appearance as do the staggered dual exhaust pipes. Fender trim, dash, running lights, turn signals, mirrors and headlight have all been updated where necessary to conform to highway legislation as well as enhancing appearance, but remain traditional Harley-Davidson. By 1996, the FLSTC Heritage Softail Classic was being

offered.

The Heritage Softail Classic is another of Harley-Davidson's contemporary, though nostalgic, dresser-style motorcycles. Its Hardtail frame styling, together with the use of the Softail frame in conjunction with hydraulic telescopic front forks, is in many ways the fifties Hydra-Glide reincarnated for the nineties. Unlike the Hydra-Glide, though, the Heritage Softail Classic came along with refinements to its rear suspension such as electric start, belt drive, disc brakes front and rear, and the larger-capacity Evolution V-twin. Despite such modern components the styling is unmistakably big, old Harley-Davidson; the big valanced FL fenders, shrouded forks on which the headlights, additional spotlights and windshield brackets are mounted, the wide dresser bars, timeless fatbob tank that follows into a studded leather seat and the large studded saddlebags all contribute to this appearance. The end result is the best of both worlds, modern convenience, comfort and speed and the classic style of an altogether different decade.

The Fat Boy was something completely different. It was an unusually named and styled motorcycle and moved the factory custom concept in a new direction. It first appeared in 1990 and mechanically was a Softail but with cast alloy 16-inch disc wheels, fully valanced front fender, shotgun exhaust pipes and wide FLH bars. In the first year the Fat Boy – the FLSTF – was available in silver metallic paint with yellow detailing. Subsequently, having become an established model in the Harley range, it was offered in a variety of colours. On its introduction, FLSTF Fat Boy caused a stir for several reasons, not least of which was its unusual name. It also caused a stir because of its unusual appearance – it was a factory custom from a completely different mould. Its appearance was of a heavyweight solid motorcycle with its squat stance and solid cast alloy wheels. The first models were only available in grey but since then the Fat Boy has become a regular in the Harley-Davidson range and is now sold in a number of different colours. The FLSTF Fat Boy somehow projects an old-style look while being completely modern: its overall shape could be considered almost vintage but for its solid wheels, Evolution engine and custom-style parts, including the front fender and shotgun

dual exhaust pipes.

Alongside the Softail range came the FXR range – the R suffix designating a rubber-mounted engine and a redesigned frame. It was a continuation of the series that began in 1982 with the Shovelhead-powered FXR and FXRS. By 1987, the FXRs were acknowledged to be better machines than the rigid mount FXs: so Harley-Davidson combined the FXR with the chopper look of the FX. The result was a V2-powered, five-speed, belt-drive motorcycle with a solid rear wheel, a 21-inch front wheel, an XR1000 front fender and a small XL-type headlight. It was referred to as the FXLR – FX Low Rider Custom. For 1989 there was a logical extension to the FXR range, the FXR Low Rider Convertible. It converted from a Low Rider custom to a touring bike through the use of removable saddlebags and windshield. The model was popular, the 1992 FXRS Convertible, one of the FXR Series of Big Twin Evolution models, was a modern motorcycle with a number of factory custom styling touches and include the FXR Super Glide, FXRS-SP Low Rider Sport, FXLR Low Rider Custom and the FXRS-Conv as seen here. All the FXR models feature rubber-mounted engines, five-speed transmissions and belt final drives. The result of this combination is a smooth and vibration-free motorcycle. The FXRS-Conv is seen as a versatile sport touring machine. To make it suitable for touring it has such refinements as air-adjustable front suspension through a chamber inside the handlebars, a removable Lexan windshield and removable saddlebags made from nylon and leather. It is suitable for fitting a Harley-Davidson sidecar. The model shown here has been further personalized by its owner who has incorporated a number of custom inspection and aircleaner covers as well as custom gas caps, a luggage rack and turn signal ornaments. It was still in Harley's

A special limited-edition FXRS was built for the 50th anniversaries of the two biggest bike rallies in the U.S.A. – Sturgis and Daytona. This is the Daytona Anniversary model of which less than 2,000 examples were made.

range in 1996 as the FXDS Conv Dyna Convertible.

The frame used in Dyna Glide models was re-engineered for the 1996 models to lower the motorcycle and although it is a traditional-looking motorcycle the FXDS Conv does not convey the same feeling of nostalgia as several of the other models in the nineties model ranges. It is more of a dual purpose bike for both cruising and touring. The windshield and panniers are designed to be quickly removable to allow the motorcycle to change roles. The Evolution engine is rubber-mounted to minimize the passage of vibration through to rider and pillion The Dyna Convertible originated from the Super Glide, hence the FX prefix to its model designation. The Super Glide remains in the range as a basic and traditional big twin Harley, featuring the Dyna frame and Evolution engine but with traditional telescopic forks and spoked wheels. The Dyna Convertible has cast 13-spoke wheels and other touring accessories such as a pillion backrest.

The earlier variants were followed in 1991 by the Dyna Glide. This was introduced along with the FXDB Sturgis, named after one of America's biggest biker gatherings which celebrated its 50th anniversary in 1991. There had previously been a Shovelhead-powered belt-drive Sturgis ten years before. This Harley is also based around a new frame and some saw it as the most significant new Harley to come out in almost a decade. It ran the quarter mile in 13.58 seconds. The FXDB designation indicated Super Glide (FX), Dyna Glide chassis (D) and belt drive (B). The 50th-Anniversary Sturgis was followed by a 50th-Anniversary Daytona model. This was also an FXDB and limited to less than 2,000 models which went on sale in August 1991 as Harley's first 1992 model although it had been shown during the 50th Anniversary of the races at Daytona in Florida's Bikeweek in March. Since then, there have been other models such as the FXDC, a custom Dyna Glide and the FXSTSB. The FXSTSB Bad Boy – another unusually named motorcycle – was as close as a major factory could come to building a chopper. It features a Softail frame, springer forks, a bobbed rear fender and an old-fashioned-looking scalloped custom paint job. The 1996 FXSTSB Bad Boy is Harley's most extreme

Above
All the current Big Twin Harleys are powered by the Evolution V2 engine for which there are two types of mounting, rigid and rubber mount.

Opposite
The Road King is one of Harley's contemporary FLH models and designed along the lines of a traditional machine. The windshield and passenger seat are both removable.

factory custom to date. In many ways it is more than a factory custom, it is a full 'factory chopper'. Harley-Davidson admits, in some of its advertising, that a little notoriety has crept into its history. The film *The Wild One*, for example, was based on incidents alleged to have taken place in the town of Hollister, California, after the Second World War. Many of the riders in Hollister rode similar bikes that appear in current reincarnations. Back then, almost 50 years ago, bobbers were ridden, many of which featured shortened fenders, springer forks and had a stripped-down minimal look. The bikes were based on Knuckleheads and Flatheads but Harley, ever-conscious of its history and her-

itage, introduced the Bad Boy based around a Softail frame and Evolution engine.

Nowadays, Harley-Davidson never hesitates to take a look at what custom builders are doing to its products before offering its own interpretation of any particular style. The work of the unofficial stylist is, of course, beyond the scope of worldwide legislation which could be applied to a major motorcycle manufacturer such as Harley-Davidson: however, the factory offers acceptably styled factory customs. The 1996 FXSTS Softail Custom is such a bike; it unashamedly resembles a neatly customized creation rather than a stock bike. Based around the Softail frame, it offers Hardtail styling with

The big Electra Glides are very much at home on the road such as this one (above) seen on the road to Sturgis, South Dakota.

Opposite
The 1997 FLHT is the standard Electra Glide. It returns 50 mpg (18 km/litre) on the highway or 40 mpg in city use. The FLHT is based around a steel swing-arm frame rather than a Softail and features air-adjustable suspension.

the benefit of rear suspension. A bobbed rear fender, stepped seat, fatbob tank, raked-out front end, forward control pegs and foot pedals, a minimal front fender and big pullback bars are the definitive aftermarket parts necessary to build a custom big twin. The solid alloy rear wheel is a more modern custom style part. Harley-Davidson has collected these parts and assembled them around a Big Twin Evolution engine and five-speed transmission and offers the custom bike straight off the dealer's showroom floor.

The 1995 FXDWG Dyna Wide Glide is another production Harley-Davidson which can be described as a factory custom. Its origins are pure chopper and Harley's designers, looking at the kind of modifications being made to stock bikes, then produced their interpretation of a modified stock bike. The front end is raked out and fitted with a 21-inch front wheel, the handlebars are ape-hangers, a small front fender is fitted and a bobbed rear one. These were and still are popular custom modifications necessary to

build a custom Harley – so within certain limits Harley offered its own. There were limits: because the machine is made by a large company it has to meet the various legislation around the world. Many custom builders, for example, would not fit a front fender but the factory must. The Wide Glide designation refers to the fact that the fork legs are more widely spaced on this model than on other Big Twin Harleys.

Despite all the alterations to the FX, FXR and FLST models, the more standard-looking Big Twins, such as the Electra Glides, were not ignored. Having been upgraded through the use of the V2 Evolution engine, it was fine tuned for each model year; the 1984 and 1985 FLHT Electra Glide had a lower seat for the rider, stepped for the pillion, and a variation on the normal glass fibre fairing was fitted. The 1985 models were five speed and had final-belt drive and a new clutch. For 1987 there was a new model, the FLHS Electra Glide Sport, which was at the bottom of the Electra Glide range in terms of price

and featured a windshield rather than a fairing. Two years later another two new models were added to the line-up, the FLTC Tour Glide Ultra Classic and the FLHTC Electra Glide Ultra Classic. Both these models endured in the range and by the mid-nineties the latter were available with sequential port fuel injection systems. The FLHTC Ultra Classic models are available in both carburettor and fuel injection models, the injection models being designated FLHTCUI.

The Ultra Classic Electra Glide Injection is physically the biggest of Harley Davidson's current range of motorcycles. It is also one of the most well appointed because, although its frame and engine are similar to other models in the range, it comes with a sound system, cigarette lighter, cruise control and more instrumentation than other models. Much of this is contained within the fork-mounted fairing. The tank-mounted dash is used as the cover for the filler cap. The FLHTC in both carburettor and injection forms is also fitted with legshields – termed lowers by Harley-

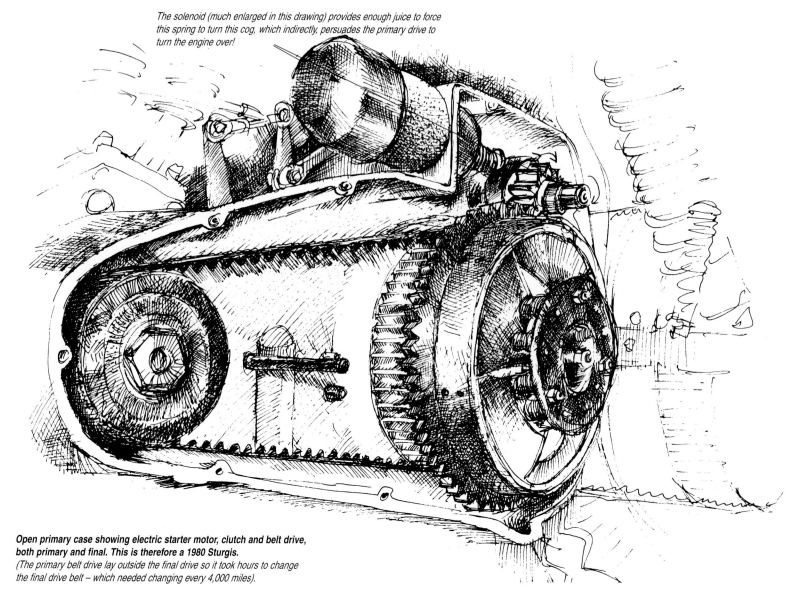

The solenoid (much enlarged in this drawing) provides enough juice to force this spring to turn this cog, which indirectly, persuades the primary drive to turn the engine over!

Open primary case showing electric starter motor, clutch and belt drive, both primary and final. This is therefore a 1980 Sturgis.
(The primary belt drive lay outside the final drive so it took hours to change the final drive belt – which needed changing every 4,000 miles).

Davidson – in which the speakers for the stereo are located. There are also rear speakers and separate controls for the passenger. The hard saddlebags are complemented by the Tour Pack in which turn signals are incorporated and on which the dual antennae for radio and CB are mounted. The Ultra Classic Tour Glide is a similar model on which the most visual innovation is the use of a differently shaped fairing. New for 1997 is the Ol' Boy, another unusually named Harley and another Big Twin with a trace of nostalgia about it is the FLSTS Heritage Springer.

The 1996 FLSTN Heritage Softail Special is yet another contemporary nostalgic Harley-Davidson based around the Softail frame and Evolution big twin engine. While it features such classic items as partially shrouded telescopic forks and 16-inch whitewall tyres back and front, it is not such a nostalgic dresser as the Heritage Softail Classic but, nonetheless, is reminiscent of an early fifties Hydra-Glide, albeit a slightly customized one. The lines of the FL fenders are unmistakable and the Softail frame gives a rigid frame appearance – it takes more than a glance to spot the pivot for the rear portion of the frame (it is actually between the exhaust pipes behind the gearbox). The chromed oil tank and other components, together with two-tone paint, provide the custom appearance, as do the staggered dual exhaust pipes. Fender trim, dash, running lights, turn signals, mirrors and headlight have all been updated where necessary to conform to highway legislation and in some cases to improve appearance while retaining the traditional Harley-Davidson look.

The mighty Electra Glide has been in production since 1965, sequentially updated and still made in standard form as the FLHT Electra Glide Standard. In its state-of-the-art 1996 form, it is refined and sophisticated but still remains a big touring motorcycle. In view of its role as a tourer the comfort of rider and pillion has been treated as a matter of

Technical Specification 1986 FXST SOFTAIL

Capacity	80 cu in (1340cc)
Engine Cycle	Four stroke
Engine Type	V-twin Evolution
Valve configuration	Overhead valve
Top Speed	112 mph (180 km/h)
Power	67 bhp @ 5000 rpm
Transmission	Four speed
Frame	Steel Softail

Technical Specification 1991 FLSTF FAT BOY	
Capacity	80 cu in (1340cc)
Engine Cycle	Four stroke
Engine Type	V-twin Evolution
Valve configuration	Overhead valve
Top Speed	115 mph (185 km/h)
Power	58 bhp @ 5000 rpm
Transmission	Five speed
Frame	Steel Softail

Technical Specification 1995 FXSTS BAD BOY	
Capacity	80 cu in (1340cc)
Engine Cycle	Four stroke
Engine Type	V-twin Evolution
Valve configuration	Overhead valve
Top Speed	120 mph (195 km/h)
Power	58 bhp @ 5000 rpm
Transmission	Five speed
Frame	Softail cradle

considerable importance, not least in the size and depth of the seats and the fact that footboards are fitted for both rider and passenger. The engine is described by Harley-Davidson as isolation-mounted to minimize vibration transmitted from the V-twin to passengers aboard. A fork-mounted fairing makes distance riding more comfortable, as does the air suspension which enables the occupants of the Electra Glide to travel and carry baggage

The Heritage Softail of 1988 was very much a fifties-inspired design of Harley-Davidson Big Twin motorcycle, redesigned for modern roads and traffic conditions and to sell to the rapidly growing nostalgia market. It featured the Softail frame, which was Harley-designed and looked like a traditional rigid frame but featured rear suspension to increase the rider and passenger's comfort.

in two capacious panniers fitted one on either side of the rear fender and on the luggage rack above which is also designed for load carrying, either with a Tour Pack fitted or simply by strapping bags to the rack.

The Softail was a restyled Big Twin from the Harley Davidson factory. Its engine was the Evolution which had been introduced in 1983/84. It first appeared in the FX models and spread across the range over the following three years. In traditional swing-arm models, the engine was rubber-mounted to minimize vibration. The Softails take their styling from an earlier age and appear to be rigid framed as the suspension is hidden. The Softails feature a chrome horseshoe oil tank and traditional fenders. One model – the FXSTS – takes nostalgia a step further and has springer forks. The Evolution and the Softail styling have made Harley-Davidson motorcycles huge sellers in the late eighties and nineties.

The Fat Boy was heralded as a spectacular motorcycle when it was unveiled. It featured solid 16-inch diameter wheels back and front and Evolution engine power in a Softail frame all added together to produce a solid appearance. Its unusual name caught on quickly and since then Harley-Davidson has named another of its range the Bad Boy.

The Harley Bad Boy is guaranteed to inspire feelings of nostalgia for times past featuring as it does the Softail frame with that old, classic look about it, Springer forks which, until the FXSTS, had not been fitted since 1948, and a hot-rod paint scheme harking back to the past. As well as these old-style features, it has up-to-date ones, too, including the Evolution engine and disc brakes.

A 1997 FXSTSB, the factory custom Bad Boy, an FX Softail Springer.

Chapter Six
THE SPORTSTER

The KH was a developed version of the K-model which itself was in some way an updated WL. The K-model was a unit construction sidevalve V-twin, built with foot-change hand clutch transmission and aimed at competing with the British bikes imported to Europe in the years after the Second World War. The main drawback of the K-model was that its performance failed to match that of the imports, so in 1954 the KH was introduced. It was a K-model engine with a lengthened stroke which meant that its displacement was increased to 883cc (54 cu in). It also had new flywheels, cylinder barrels, an improved clutch and was overall a better motorcycle and one fit to compete with the British imports on more even terms. It remained in production until 1956 when it

was replaced by the models designated XL, the first of the motorcycles referred to as Sportsters.

The K-model resembled its foreign competitors in styling in that it had a swinging arm rear suspension assembly, telescopic

The Sportster name was not used until the unit construction flathead K-models (diagram) were superseded by ohv versions (opposite). The K-model flathead is seen here in dirt track race trim while the Sportster is seen in roadgoing fform. The model name was incorporated into the primary cover and fender trim (left).

Pages 72-73
Above
A dirt track racing XR750.
Below
A 1977 Sportster XLCR.

Pages 74-75
A 1984 XR1000.

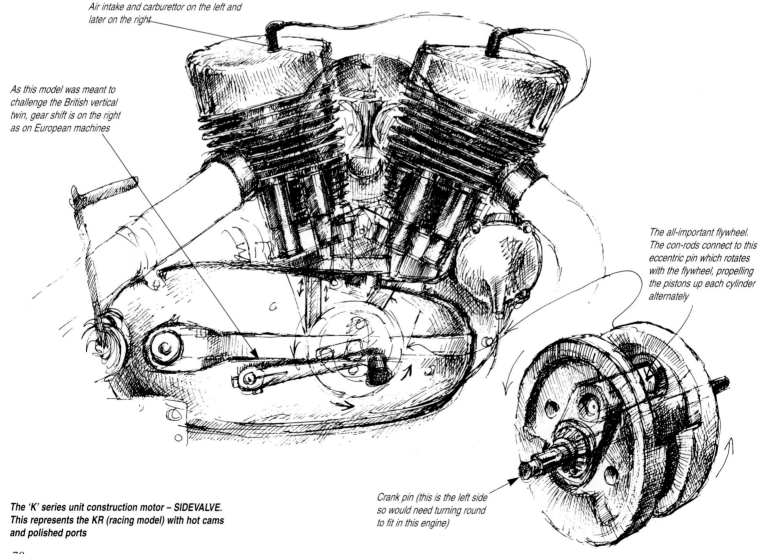

Air intake and carburettor on the left and later on the right

As this model was meant to challenge the British vertical twin, gear shift is on the right as on European machines

The all-important flywheel. The con-rods connect to this eccentric pin which rotates with the flywheel, propelling the pistons up each cylinder alternately

The 'K' series unit construction motor – SIDEVALVE. This represents the KR (racing model) with hot cams and polished ports

Crank pin (this is the left side so would need turning round to fit in this engine)

forks, foot-shift gearchange and neat compact lines. The sidevalve engine was of unit construction but was vastly slower than the imports and the KK-model was introduced in response to criticisms concerning the speed of the K-model. The KH-model was introduced a couple of years later with an enlarged capacity, 883-cc engine capable of 95mph (153 km/h). Sidevalves were becoming decidedly old-fashioned by the late fifties and were being quickly superseded by overhead valve engines.

The first XL Sportster engine displaced 883cc, although by the early seventies there was a 1000cc available in a range of models such as the XL, XLCH, XLT, XLX, among others, which stayed in production until the introduction of the Evolution-engined Sportsters in 1986. Unlike the Big Twin Harleys, Sportsters feature 'unit' construction meaning that the engine and gearbox are both part of one casting rather than two separate items. The earlier Sportsters were noted for being fast yet fragile, although these characteristics were modified as the years passed. The Sportster received a redesign in 1978 when it was given a new frame. One Sportster notable for being different from the others in the range was the XLCR of 1977. It was an XL Sportster with café racer styling, hence the CR suffix to the designation. This was an attempt to put contemporary race styling onto the street: it was not a particularly popular motorcycle at the time which means that such machines are now highly desirable to collectors and enthusiasts alike. In late 1977, Harley-Davidson introduced the radically restyled Sportster; it featured European café racer styling which basically gave it racetrack looks for the street. The CR suffix to the XL Sportster designation stood for Café Racer and was prominently displayed on the primary cover. The new Sportster was gloss black all over with the exception of the siamesed exhaust pipes which were matt black. The remainder of the bike was finished in chrome and polished alloy. Items such as the gas tank had been redesigned and the seat was clearly race track-inspired. The rear portion of the frame was based on the styling of the XR750 but the whole unit was stretched to allow the oil tank and battery to be fitted, as a result of which the shock absorbers were mounted further

Technical Specification 1977 XLCR	
Capacity	60.8 cu in (997cc)
Engine Cycle	Four stroke
Engine Type	V-twin Ironhead
Valve configuration	Overhead valve
Top Speed	124 mph (200 km/h)
Power	61 bhp @ 6200 rpm
Transmission	Four speed
Frame	Tubular steel

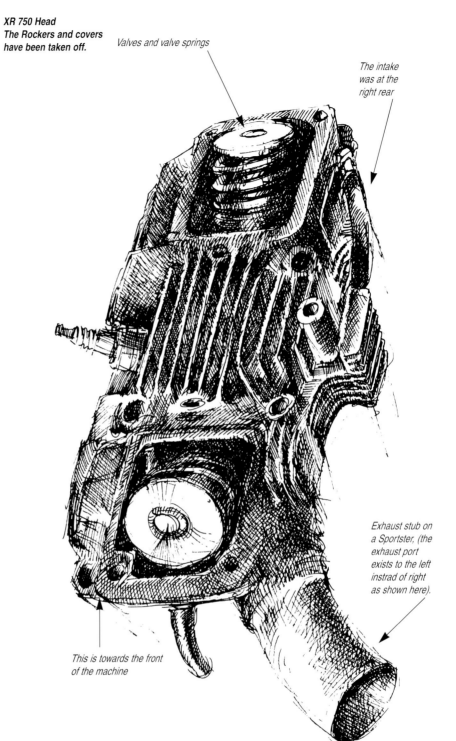

XR 750 Head
The Rockers and covers have been taken off.

Valves and valve springs

The intake was at the right rear

Exhaust stub on a Sportster, (the exhaust port exists to the left instrad of right as shown here).

This is towards the front of the machine

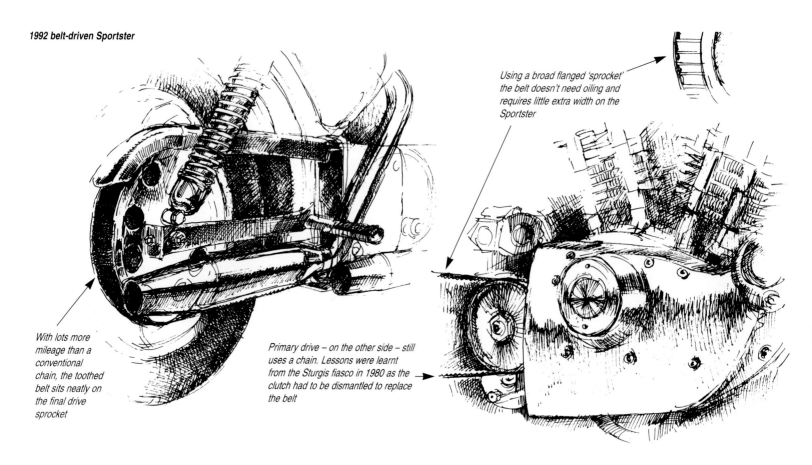

Using a broad flanged 'sprocket' the belt doesn't need oiling and requires little extra width on the Sportster

With lots more mileage than a conventional chain, the toothed belt sits neatly on the final drive sprocket

Primary drive – on the other side – still uses a chain. Lessons were learnt from the Sturgis fiasco in 1980 as the clutch had to be dismantled to replace the belt

back than on other models. Rear-set brake and gearchange mechanisms allowed the rider to assume a sportsbike riding position and cast alloy Morris wheels and Kelsey

Technical Specification 1978 XR750	
Capacity	45 cu in (748cc)
Engine Cycle	Four stroke
Engine Type	V-twin Ironhead
Valve configuration	Overhead valve
Top Speed	130 mph (210 km/h) (dependent on gearing)
Power	79-90 bhp @ 6200 rpm (dependent on tune)
Transmission	Four speed
Frame	Tubular steel

Hayes disc brakes completed the sporting appearance. The XL Sportster was the basis of Harley-Davidson's competition bikes and evolved with the popularity of dirt track and flat track racing among popular forms of competitive motorcycling in the United States.

The XLCR was a special limited-edition version of the Sportster of which only 3,000 were ever made. The XLCR was a café racer-styled Sportster with a nose fairing and alloy wheels. It was based around a derivative of the race-proven XR750 frame; it was lengthened, and was powered by a 997-cc Ironhead Sportster engine.

In 1969 the rules governing dirt track racing in the United States were altered. Class C dirt track was from then on for production 750s, be the engines sidevalve or overhead. As a result, Harley-Davidson's racing department had to find a replacement racer for the KR sidevalve machines in order to keep the marque competitive on the dirt ovals around the U.S.A. The internals of the engine were considerably different to the XR models for street use. The flywheels were different as was much of the rest of the engine. Iron components failed to dissipate the heat sufficiently for racing purposes so, later on, the factory built an alloy version of the XR750. The revised format was far more successful for racing and the bike went on to

Technical Specification
1984 XR1000

Capacity	61 cu in (998cc)
Engine Cycle	Four stroke
Engine Type	V-twin Ironhead
Valve configuration	Overhead valve
Top Speed	120 mph (193 km/h)
Power	70 bhp @ 6000rpm
Transmission	Four speed
Frame	Tubular cradle

become a legend of the dirt tracks, especially when ridden by men like Jay Springsteen, Ricky Graham, Scott Parker and Chris Carr.

This was a bike built by Harley-Davidson for racing, initially on dirt tracks and based loosely on many of the components of the XL series of Sportsters – hence its XR designation; X from the Sportster, R for racing. It used a unit construction 45-degree V-twin engine and gearbox and initially was styled along similar lines to the KR-models. At first the XR750 used an iron engine but after numerous problems, with heat dissipation among others, the XR750 was manufactured with an alloy engine. It became a racing legend.

As a result of the popularity of such racing, competition-inspired models such as the XR1000 featured in Harley's range in 1983. The 1983 XR1000 was a competition-type bike manufactured and marketed for the street. In many ways it was a styling exercise as the bike was a mixture of Sportster

XL1000 street parts and XR750 race parts. The engine used an XL1000 bottom end with cylinder heads, exhausts and carburettors from the XR750 racing engine. The barrels were new components. The dual carburettors were positioned on the right side of the engine and the exhaust pipes on the left. The remainder of the machine was almost all the then stock XLX Sportster which was really the basic model. Because the XR1000 was a limited-edition model and made from an unusual combination of parts, it retailed for a higher price than the other Sportsters in the early eighties range. Despite this, it was a fast motorcycle and the first Harley to achieve drag strip quarter-mile times of less than 13 seconds.

1984 XR1000

The XR1000 was an exercise in both engineering and marketing in that it was the closest thing to a race bike the man in the street could buy. The engine was derived from the XR750 racer with a Sportster XL1000 bottom end and a set of iron cylinders and alloy heads. Dual carburettors were fitted on the right of the engine and twin exhausts on the left. The remainder of the bike was the basic XLX Sportster.

In 1986, the Evolution-engined Sportster made its appearance as an 883-cc displace-

ment machine; then the range was enlarged with the addition of an 1100-cc model which was subsequently increased to 1200cc displacement. The new engine components were notable for reducing wear and oil consumption in the Sportster models. The transmission was upgraded from four speed to five speed to take advantage of the better engine and follow the worldwide trend towards five- and six-speed motorcycles. The 883 Sportster is the model with the smallest displacement in the Harley-Davidson range (53.8 cu in) and

Technical Specification
1991 XLH

Capacity	53.8 cu in (883cc)
Engine Cycle	Four stroke
Engine Type	V-twin Evolution
Valve configuration	Overhead valve
Top Speed	110 mph (185 km/h)
Power	49 bhp @ 6000rpm
Transmission	Five speed
Frame	Tubular steel

Above
An 883 Sportster competing in the U.S. Twinsports series, a championship for 883-cc Sportsters supported by the Harley-Davidson factory.

Opposite far right
The tank badge and aircleaner of the KH-model flat-head, forerunner to the ohv Sportster. Harley-Davidson has always emphasized its use of the V-twin configuration engines.

the model designation reflects the metric displacement. It is also the smallest model in the range in terms of weight and length. The 883 model is one of a number of Sportster variants, including 1200-cc models. There are basic, custom and competition-inspired models marketed and variations in components, particularly types of seats and wheels, are used to enhance these themes. Overall the Sportster is a traditional motorcycle that has been sequentially upgraded through its long production run. The 1996 model is powered by the proven Evolution V2 engine with a five-speed transmission and belt final drive. The latter feature was newly introduced in 1993.

Around the world there are race series for the 883 model Sportsters on both surfaced and unsurfaced tracks; the 883 is used as the basis for dirt track race bikes in an exclusively Harley-Davidson 883 series which runs concurrently with the American Motorcycle Association-sanctioned 750 class in Grand National events. There are also a series of surfaced track races exclusive to 883cc Sportsters such as U.S. Twinsports.

Based on the success of the various Sportster circuit racing series around the world and the proven dirt and flat track her-

itage of the Sportster, a new model appeared for 1996. It is the XL1200S Sportster 1200 Sport. The nimble new model features a number of performance parts such as the gas-assisted rear shock absorbers and cartridge-type damper valving on the front forks, thereby making the machine's entire suspension adjustable. The front end also features twin floating disc brakes and a disc rear brake. The styling reflects the bike's sporting aspirations; a pair of flat track-style handlebars, the redesigned 3.3-gallon gas tank and a dual sports seat are complemented by the 13-spoke cast wheels. The racing origins and performance aspect of the machine is underlined by the tank badge, the manufacturer's name, Harley-Davidson, being prominent (so too, is a V logo referring to the legendary V-twin) and a panel of race-style chequer pattern completes the design.

Harley-Davidson, aware of the heritage of the smaller-capacity Sportster models, introduced the 1200 custom model as a new addition to the range for 1996. The redesigned model enhances the Sportster's lean lines. The suspension was lowered, a redesigned 3.3-gallon gas tank and new emblem and custom-style seat are all fitted. Also selected to give a custom appearance are the chromed

bullet headlight, low rise handlebars and tall risers. The controls on the handlebars are less cluttered than in previous years and much more of the wiring has been concealed. A 21-inch front wheel and 16-inch rear are standard custom fare although in the fashion of the nineties the front is of traditional spoked design while the rear is of tough slotted alloy. Belt drive and disc brakes give a finishing touch to the Sportster, in mechanical terms, while a selection of paint schemes complete the machine's appearance.

A new model, sharing little with the existing Sportsters beyond its displacement, made its début at Daytona one spring. It was the VR1000, a liquid-cooled racing bike. The machine has been raced at numerous events and, although success has so far eluded it, there is much speculation that the VR1000 may be a rolling testbed for a new generation of Harley-Davidsons: it is not unlikely that increasingly stringent noise and emissions regulations will make the production of air-cooled motorcycles impossible in the fore-seeable future.

1991 XLH Sportster

While much of Harley's range is based around the 1340-cc (80-cu in) so-called Big Twin Evolution engine, the company has another range in production. The Sportster range is based around a unit construction engine of which two displacements are available, the 883- and 1200-cc (54- and 73.2-cu in) versions. The 883 is perceived by many as an entry level Harley but its success on race tracks and the fact that there are specific race series for this model indicate otherwise.

1996 XLH Sportster Hugger

Of the Harley-Davidson range, the 883 Sportster is the model with the smallest displacement (53.8 cu in) and the model designation reflects the metric displacement. It is also the smallest model in the range in terms of weight and length. The 1996 model is powered by the proven Evolution V2 engine with a five-speed transmission and belt final drive.

Technical Specification 1996 XLH

Capacity	53.8 cu in (883cc)
Engine Cycle	Four stroke
Engine Type	V-twin Evolution
Valve configuration	Overhead valve
Top Speed	110 mph (185 km/h)
Power	61 Nm @ 2500 rpm
Transmission	Five speed
Frame	Tubular steel

A 1996 XL1200S Sportster 1200 Sport. This machine is based on the success of the various Sportster racing events and its proven dirt and flat track heritage. It uses the unit construction 1200-cc Evolution Sportster engine and a steel swing-arm frame fitted with telescopic forks. Twin disc front brakes and gas-assisted shock absorbers reflect the bike's sporting origins.

Index

Page numbers in *italics* refer to illustrations